LINDA W. WAGNER is widely known for her work in twentieth-century American literature. Professor of English at Michigan State University, she is the author of *Dos Passos: Artist as American*, also published by the University of Texas Press, and of studies of Hemingway, Faulkner, and William Carlos Williams.

ELLEN GLASGOW

Ellen Glasgow

BEYOND CONVENTION

by Linda W. Wagner

UNIVERSITY OF TEXAS PRESS, AUSTIN

Requests for permission to reproduce material
from this work should be sent to Permissions,
University of Texas Press, Box 7819, Austin, Texas 78712.

LIBRARY OF CONGRESS CATALOGING IN PUBLICATION DATA
Wagner, Linda Welshimer.
Ellen Glasgow, beyond convention.
Bibliography: p.
Includes index.
1. Glasgow, Ellen Anderson Gholson, 1873–1945—
Criticism and interpretation.   I. Title.
PS3513.L34Z98   813'.52   82-2067   AACR2
ISBN 0-292-72039-4

Frontispiece courtesy of the Ellen Glasgow Papers,
Manuscripts Department, University of Virginia Library.

I am indebted to my good friends Nancy Ainsworth,
Dorothy Scura, and Cathy N. Davidson
for their support and professionalism
and to my students in women's literature
for their continuing enthusiasm.

Contents

Preface

Ellen Glasgow was a writer important to both the main direction of modern American fiction and that of literature written by women. She began her career before the turn of the century, when being mistaken for a male writer was considered the highest praise. Her earliest fiction—*The Descendant*, 1897; *Phases of an Inferior Planet*, 1898; *The Voice of the People*, 1900—portrays male protagonists overcoming inimical circumstance; the strong female characters included early in these novels usually disappeared midway through the books. All attention, all interest, lay in the male protagonist.

Glasgow's writing career (1897 through her death in 1945) shows a gradual change in her self-image, a change which is reflected in voice and character throughout her nineteen novels. The imitative, pseudo-masculine voice gives way to a feminine perspective. Female characters become more significant, and their philosophies central to fictional theme. By the time of *Virginia*, 1913, Glasgow has dropped her earlier condescending attitude toward women and writes with evocative sympathy about her female characters. And her style correspondingly becomes less didactic, more highly imaged, as though she wants to employ more variety in techniques to move her readers.

Not surprisingly, Glasgow's best writing comes late in her career. When she wrote *Barren Ground* in 1925, she was nearing fifty, and the trilogy of manners—*The Romantic Comedians*, 1926; *They Stooped to Folly*, 1929; and *The Sheltered Life*, 1932—were the fruit of her maturity. One suspects, in reading her fiction, that Glasgow's values changed throughout her lifetime as she learned the variety of human experience. She was no longer content to imitate fashionable male novelists; instead, in these late novels, Glasgow had the conviction about her characters to make them live. Their existence was crucial to her. She wrote with more power than ever before.

My approach in *Ellen Glasgow: Beyond Convention* is to relate Glasgow's own life experiences to the maturity of her fiction. This study is a continuation of the work of Monique Parent (Frazee), whose 1962 book *Ellen Glasgow: Romancière*, recognized Glasgow as a woman writer in a culture marked by rapidly changing attitudes toward professional women. This 1962 book is available only in French; it also follows the pattern of much French criticism in that it treats many critical problems exhaustively. My short book is intended only to introduce the reader to Ellen Glasgow, her work, and the Southern and American culture from which she developed.

ELLEN GLASGOW

Below the animated surface, I was already immersed
in some dark stream of identity, stronger and deeper and
more relentless than the external movement of living.
It was not that I had so early found my vocation. At the age of
seven my vocation had found me. The one permanent interest,
the single core of unity at the center of my nature,
was beginning to shape itself, and to harden. I was born
a novelist, though I formed myself into an artist.
—Ellen Glasgow, *The Woman Within*

CHAPTER I

The Sense of Exile

As writer and as woman, Ellen Glasgow managed to exist within the cultural and literary confines of her age, and yet to live and write as she wanted. This accomplishment—even for today—is not small. Indeed, for a woman born in 1873 to a protective Virginia family, the accomplishment seems overwhelming.

Glasgow achieved her status as an important American novelist—recipient of the 1942 Pulitzer Prize for Fiction and numerous other awards—through a lifetime of dedication to the craft of writing. That dedication, however, was hard won: the vivacious Glasgow knew well the temptation of the typical womanly life. Engaged several times,[1] she spent most of her life walking a tightrope between one identity as a desirable woman and another as an ambitious and therefore forbidding female author. The two roles, for her day, seemed irreconcilable, and the tensions the impasse caused may have created the force behind some of her best writing. During the later years of her career, Glasgow was at her finest writing fiction about women, women whose lives were markedly unconventional.

She said, simply, that she liked to write about women because "their complexity interested" her.[2] Yet as Erich Kahler and others have shown, most writing results from a need to acquire self-knowledge, to explore the intimate self. As Kahler phrases it, "Man himself has developed by means of the perpetual interaction between consciousness and reality, between his interior world and his exterior world. . . . By his efforts to organize that world he becomes aware of his own inner world as a coherent self. By objectification of the outer world he takes possession of his inner world." Glasgow also describes a similar process:

> A novelist must write, not by taking thought alone, but with every cell of his being . . . nothing can occur to him that may not sooner or later find its way into his craft . . . everything one has seen or heard or thought or felt leaves a deposit that never filters entirely through the essence of mind.[3]

Most readers would accept the generalization that Glasgow was interested in women characters at least partly because she was herself a woman. In her fiction, and in the countless characterizations of women that that fiction included, Glasgow was able to portray, define, and then redefine the essential female qualities—as well as the matrix in which they flourished or hungered. Her interest in this process stemmed partly from the fact that she was an ironist: she was amused by the differences between the traditional concepts of woman and her own personal concepts. Cautiously defiant, Glasgow as a woman of the late nineteenth century knew well how much of a rebel she had become. One has only to contrast her own life—from the mysterious affair with a married man through friendships with Thomas Hardy, Hugh Walpole, and other literary lions to her last engagement to a Southern lawyer—with her vivid description of the normal condition of womanhood:

> The Victorian era, above all, was one of waiting, as hell is an eternity of waiting.
> Women waiting for the first word of love from their lovers. Women waiting with all the inherited belief in the omnipotence of love, for the birth of their sons. Women waiting, during the civil war, for news of their sons and husbands. Women waiting beside the beds of the sick and dying—waiting—waiting—.
> As a result I think it is almost impossible to over-estimate the part that religion, in one form or another, has played in the lives of southern women. Nothing else could have made them accept with meekness the wing of the chicken and the double standard of morals.[4]

The contrast between the expected female role and the life Glasgow chose to lead provided her with plenty of material for her fiction. Literary criticism has only recently begun to create terminology for those conflicts. During the 1970's, studies by Kate Millett, Patricia Meyer Spacks, Adrienne Rich, Ellen Moers, Annis V. Pratt, and others attempted to show the problems inherent in being female writers. The fullest statement available is Sandra Gilbert and Susan Gubar's *The Madwoman in the Attic: The Woman Writer and the Nineteenth Century Literary Imagination*. And as Carolyn Heilbrun has recently said,

> Men have monopolized human experience, leaving women unable to imagine themselves as both ambitious and female. If I imagine myself (woman has always asked) whole, active, a self, will I not cease, in some profound way, to be a woman? . . . Literature is

both the fruit and the nourishment of the imagination. We must look to it not only for the articulation of female despair and constriction, but also for the proclamation of the possibilities of life. We must ask women writers to give us, finally, female characters who are complex, whole, and independent—fully human.[5]

That such characters do exist in Glasgow's fiction reflects at least in part the strength of her will to succeed on her own terms as a woman writer. Glasgow's development to the point where she could create such characters is one subject of this study.

Partly because Glasgow would accept neither the submissive stance nor the chicken wing, she maintained throughout her life a "strange sense of exile on earth": indeed, the working title for her memoirs was "The Autobiography of an Exile." For Glasgow, the conflict between having to be aggressive in order to write, and passive in order to exist, was intensified by living in the South. She wrote wistfully, "Had I been born in another country. The sense of exile. Fortunate Elinor Wylie! Had she spent her life in the South. . . ."[6]

Glasgow wrote freely in her autobiography about her sense of alienation (the book was to be published only after her death; that injunction gave her a sense of privacy). Her fiction reveals the theme just as clearly. When asked about her first story, "Only a Daisy," the product of her seventh year, Glasgow replied,

> I seem to have been born with my theme . . . the lonely daisy, the field of roses, translated into the outsider . . . the lonely newcomer, the person who does not belong entering a settled society and fighting for a place in it.[7]

Some sense of ambivalence is pictured here—not only Glasgow's being an outsider but also the urgency of belonging. Vacillate as she did between defying convention and rushing toward it, Glasgow yet speaks with pride in *The Woman Within*:

> Only on the surface of things have I ever trod the beaten path. So long as I could keep from hurting anyone else, I have lived, as completely as it was possible, the life of my choice. I have been free. . . . I have done the work I wished to do for the sake of that work alone. And I have come, at last, from the fleeting rebellion of youth into the steadfast . . . accord without surrender of the unreconciled heart.[8]

Glasgow imaged her freedom particularly in her choice of work. Her family "scoffed at area writers." As she recalled in *A Certain Measure*, "My early work was written in secret to escape ridicule, alert, pointed, and not the less destructive because it was playful. . . . When a bound copy of my first book reached me, I hid it under my pillow while a cousin, who had run in for breakfast, prattled beside my bed of the young men who had quarrelled over the privilege of taking her to the Easter German."[9] Because of the hostility of her family toward her role as writer, Glasgow explains the kind of "duality" that many artists will recognize,

> Like every other wilful author, I have led, for as many years as I can remember, a dual existence. The natural writer must, of necessity, live on the surface the life of accepted facts, which is the life of action and shadows, while with his deeper consciousness he continues to live that strangely valid life of the mind, which is related to the essence of things in themselves and to the more vivid world of the imagination. (*CM*, vii–viii)

The pressure of social acceptance and family sensibility is undoubtedly greater on daughters than on sons.

Glasgow's sense of exile was intensified early by her frail health and, later, by her deafness. As she wrote in 1909 to her friend Elizabeth Patterson, "I have been very very unhappy at times. My hearing always stands between me and everything. I can't hear, even with my acoustical . . . , and this depresses me terribly. Life is over for me, my Lizzie."[10] After many visits to specialists, Glasgow could not say she had been helped. The isolation this handicap caused was very real.

That her health was fragile from birth is also important to Glasgow's later development. "Born without a skin," as her Mammy said, she attended school infrequently (see her poignant account of early hours in a classroom, *WW*, 41–49). Her absence from school would surely have set her apart from other children. Even within her own family, Ellen was somewhat isolated. Of the eight living children, she was the seventh. The three older sisters and older brother Arthur were remote from her in age. She formed a group comprised of Frank, who committed suicide at thirty-six, and Rebe or Rebie, who married a man Ellen disliked. Her deep love for her mother and for Cary, the third sister, was an enduring force in her life, but both those women died prematurely.

Glasgow characterizes her life as "a fight for freedom from illness" and "a fight for tranquility." An equilibrium that most people could assume became the prize for Glasgow: she could assume nothing—not health, certainly, nor friendship. "For my whole life, from my earliest infancy, which I remember with extraordinary vividness, had been a struggle for inward calm, for the shining peace of contemplation in a world that seemed to me barely more than emotional chaos." [11] Because all artists translate personal experience into art, in one way or another, these facts about Glasgow's life are essential. As she wrote in a draft of *The Woman Within*,

> Imagination should re-create, but not invent out of nothing in the novel; of experience there should be at least a basis of the actuality for the subtle fancy to work over. [12]

That Glasgow's basis of actuality more and more often came from her personal experience became apparent as her novels appeared.

Glasgow's personal journey to self-knowledge was necessarily different from that of many modern women. She was born into a world ruled by an autocratic father, who lived casually by the double standard. She matured into male-dominated educational experiences and read widely under the tutelage of Walter McCormack, her beloved but unstable brother-in-law. Patricia Spacks has written about women maturing within patriarchal educational systems; [13] for Glasgow, that maturing was unusually critical. It was twenty years before she developed a sense of self that was truly feminine. Her dependence on men throughout her life—both personally and literarily—shows how thoroughly ingrained the Cinderella story was, especially in its Southern variants.

Luckily, Glasgow's strong sense of humor enabled her to see the irony in writing about women whose lives were ruined because of their dependence on men, while she still looked for her own knight, whether he was armored or Red Cross. [14] Because her struggle to be independent lasted so long, she sounds triumphant in this late note from the manuscript collection:

> I have had as much love and more romance than most women, and I have not had to stroke some man the right way to win my bread or the wrong way to win my freedom. [15]

As a woman, Glasgow had played the typical female games—dressing well, flirting, being submissive—but she had stayed clear of most intimacies. Her letters as well as her fiction show that she had, indeed, known passion and love but it is also evident that those experiences had delivered the woman in her instead of confining her. When Glasgow speaks of coming into her own at sixty, she is not feigning satisfaction.[16]

One might have thought she had found satisfaction earlier, in 1913 with the publication of *Virginia* and, in 1916, with *Life and Gabriella*. These novels analyze the role of traditional women in a tone new to Glasgow. Writing with acerbity, she was able to portray both the condition of woman during the late 1800's and the more desirable position of the achieving modern woman. She knew about the conventional woman because she had witnessed the comparatively unfulfilled lives of her mother and several of her sisters. Glasgow's mother, after bearing ten children, had discovered her husband's black mistress. Her mother's resulting breakdown is described vividly in *The Woman Within* and perhaps re-created in the actions of Mary Evelyn in *Vein of Iron*. In Glasgow's own life, she weathered the end of an affair with a married man and the deaths of many family members. Her mother's death in 1893 triggered periods of depression and impaired hearing that would plague her throughout her life. The suicide of her brother-in-law in 1894 was a recurring tragedy because it defeated his young wife Cary, who lived with the Glasgows until her own death in 1911. In 1910 Ellen's brother Frank also committed suicide.

Once Cary and Frank were dead, Glasgow moved to New York—permanently, she thought. The despair of the fruitless lives of her mother and sister, both women having had little identity aside from their roles as wives, brought passion to Glasgow's characterization of Virginia Pendleton in *Virginia*. Searching for more satisfying options for women, she then created the independent heroine Gabriella Carr. Both *Life and Gabriella* and *Virginia* suggest women's lives as Glasgow would have created them—full, satisfying, tranquil. Such a life was still a fantasy for Glasgow herself.

Returning home as she finally did in 1916, after the deaths of her father and her sister Emily, Glasgow saw herself as incomplete. At forty-three she had had an impressive career, financial security, engagements, a home; but she had not escaped all the implications of being an unmarried, and perhaps unwanted, woman. Glasgow was ready for romance, and an aspiring candidate lived not far from her.

The presence of Henry Anderson at One West Main, Richmond, Virginia, dispelled the ghosts of her family members. Anderson's love for Glasgow—continuing in some form as it did for over thirty years—satisfied many of the needs culture ascribes to romance. That there was genuine feeling in the relationship is obvious from the one-sided correspondence housed at the University of Virginia. But as Glasgow wrote in *The Woman Within*, their real love lasted but seventeen months of the twenty-odd years. Spring, 1916, to summer, 1917, was the year of passion, a year that ended with Anderson's going abroad in service to the Red Cross. His absence, in addition to the misery of World War I, seemed to destroy the relationship. The climax of the courtship had occurred in July of 1917, when they had become engaged. On July 18 Henry had written to her,

> My dearest, my dearest, my heart hurts me this morning as it feels the pain of your letter with the pain of going away. What have I done to hurt you so? What can I do to heal the wound? I am in the midst of mental confusion and don't know what to do or say— . . . *I want to see you.* . . . My dearest you are the most beautiful ideal I have ever known, and I long to be able to climb to where you dwell, not to bring you down to me. Let me talk to you tonight. Now the only words that ring in my head are "I have hurt you" "I have hurt you" "Help me to heal." I can only say the picture is the loveliest thing I ever saw. My heart thanks you, and I long to kneel before you.

That night Ellen Glasgow, forty-four-year-old writer, who had so well catalogued and chronicled the fate of the married woman, wrote an ecstatic note:

I became engaged to Henry this evening.[17]

The following day Anderson left for the grand voyage of his life, commanding the Red Cross in Rumania. Mails were slow. Glasgow appears to have suffered untoward fits of jealousy and depression throughout the winter, prompted by her suspicions of a romance between Anderson and the adventurous, beautiful Queen Marie of Rumania. Her own suspicion was objectionable to her, but the most important cause of her depression was her belief that Anderson was using the war for his personal aggrandizement. He was enjoying travel, the company of royalty, and his own position as host for countless entertainments, all under the guise of war effort. Judging from Glasgow's idealization of Anderson and his sentiments in the characterization of David Blackburn (in her 1919 *The Builders*), any tinge of self-interest on his part would be troublesome to Glasgow.

The correspondence which remains from 1918 shows some of Anderson's parallel anguish. There is, of course, Glasgow's suicide attempt on July 3 of 1918, hardly an auspicious beginning for his homecoming. By fall, when Anderson had made his plans to return to Rumania for a second winter season, the romance with Glasgow was effectively over although it ostensibly continued until Glasgow's death in 1945. What support there was in Anderson's appearing for dinner and conversation, reading the drafts of her manuscripts, and sending her jewels from Cartier's or Tiffany's at Christmas, one can only guess. The relationship which continued so long must have been at least a vestige of Glasgow's feeling that a successful woman had to somehow, in some way, have an escort.

Her working through that last long fascination of the engagement with Anderson, the period which she terms "The Years of the Locust," became the prewriting period of her 1925 novel, *Barren Ground*. The power of Dorinda Oakley's renunciation of the conventional female role came directly from Glasgow's own convictions. When she speaks of the ten years of agony which enabled her to write the book, she gives the chronology of the Anderson relationship. "I've finished with all that" is Glasgow's voice as well as Dorinda's. Only some readers find that renunciation neurotic.[18]

The process of Glasgow's coming to *Barren Ground* so nearly echoes her description of the way *Virginia* was written that we must attend the reciprocity between a writer's emotional convictions and the quality of the writing which results. Moved by sentiments she could not define, Glasgow wrote *Barren Ground* as she had written the best of her novels, because she could not help but write it. In 1902, for example, she had written to a friend about *The Deliverance*:

> And so I have begun upon another big, deep, human document which no one will understand because it is wrung from life itself—and not from sugared romance. I doubt much if even you will care for it, but I could no more help writing it than I could live and not breathe the air about me. It was this or death for me—for I had come to the final choice that some are forced to make—and when I left New York it did not seem to me within the remotest range of probabilities that I should see the New Year in upon this planet. Yet here I am, for the idea saved me.[19]

The years before *Barren Ground* are, for Glasgow, the years of the short story. In these shorter forms, she explored the process of creating strong women who were betrayed by aggressive (and often rhetorical) men. Like Corinna Page in Glasgow's *One Man in His Time* (1922), women in these stories are among the most independent she ever created. They are defiant women, choosing their own moralities (which include taking lovers and killing sick husbands), responsible to few cultural mores but motivated by deep personal integrity.

Barren Ground's Dorinda Oakley is the natural outgrowth of those short story heroines, but Glasgow has the brilliance to give Dorinda more than just independence. Dorinda succeeds not because she is female but because—of all Glasgow's characters—she has the courage to recognize her need for a continuing tradition, imaged in this novel as the land. Responsive to the human creature's need for place, Dorinda withholds nothing of herself in making her farm fruitful. That her land becomes a nurturing place, that it flourishes because Dorinda pours her energy and love into it, suggests a particularly generous kind of salvation.

Glasgow's creation of Dorinda becomes especially important when we see the character which embodies the author's personal ideal of success—a character fully realized in the fiction, fully responded to by readers of that fiction—criticized as being abnormal because some readers are not willing to accept the premises of success established by the author. To Glasgow, Dorinda Oakley was a satisfied, well-functioning human being. Yet to Glasgow's biographer, E. Stanly Godbold, Dorinda Oakley was "a mechanized human being totally drained of humanity," a character who could have been created "only by an embittered and cynical woman."[20] Carolyn Heilbrun can complain that "women writers, like successful women in male-dominated professions, have failed to imagine autonomous women characters. With remarkably few exceptions, women writers do not imagine women characters with even the autonomy they themselves have achieved."[21]

The fact is, however, that when such female characters have existed in literature—as Dorinda Oakley most assuredly does in *Barren Ground*—some readers have been quick to discount her achievements, to type the woman character portrayed as "abnormal." Phyllis Chesler has spoken of one kind of suspicion in *Women and Madness*; Mary Hiatt chronicles the critical reception of women writers in *The Way Women Write*, and suggests that censure by male critics and readers has probably been the most important deterrent to the full self-actualization of many women writers. As Elaine Showalter summarizes in *A Literature of Their Own*:

Victorian feminine novelists thus found themselves in a double bind. They felt humiliated by the condescension of male critics and spoke intensely of their desire to avoid special treatment and achieve genuine excellence, but they were deeply anxious about the possibility of appearing unwomanly. . . . In the face of this dilemma, women novelists developed several strategies, both personal and artistic. Among the personal reactions was a persistent self-deprecation of themselves as women, sometimes expressed as humility, sometimes as coy assurance-seeking, and sometimes as the purest self-hatred.[22]

Glasgow's career in its various stages illustrates Showalter's thesis in part: much of the favor-currying of which she is sometimes accused would surely have been unnecessary if she had not felt inferior, or undervalued, in the literary world. Her feeling of inferiority was hardly the result of her novels' actual commercial success. Glasgow's books sold well, consistently well, beginning with the 1900 publication of *The Voice of the People*. That novel, the 1902 *The Battle-Ground*, and *Deliverance* in 1904 were all "best sellers." The 1904 novel held second place on the year's best-seller list. In 1906 Glasgow's *The Wheel of Life* held tenth place; in 1916, *Life and Gabriella* captured fifth. In 1926, *The Romantic Comedians* was a Book-of-the-Month Club selection, and in 1929 *They Stooped to Folly* was a selection of the Literary Guild. In 1932 *The Sheltered Life* placed fifth on the best-seller annual list, in 1935 *Vein of Iron* was second on that same rating, and in 1942 Glasgow won the Pulitzer Prize for *In This Our Life*. During these years, she had also been chosen the sixth woman member of the American Academy of Arts and Letters and was awarded the elusive Howells Medal for Fiction. She had also received a special award from *The Saturday Review of Literature* and several honorary doctorates from prestigious universities. Despite all the evidence of acceptance and recognition, however, early criticism aimed at her position as "woman writer" and inadequate craftsman still rankled. Francis Hackett, for example, writing in 1909, had carped,

As one of the most conspicuous woman novelists in the country, Miss Glasgow might have been assumed to take fiction seriously, to be scrupulous especially in its technique, however vague and tenderminded in her philosophy. But it needs no practitioner to find her wanting in the results of that simple self-criticism without which no one should pretend to be a writer.[23]

Because of criticism like this, most of Glasgow's concern in her later career was to express her aesthetic position. She realized early that craft was the lever that would raise her, "woman writer" that she was, to equality with the writers she admired. She also recognized the importance of the prefaces Maxwell Perkins asked her to write during 1937 and 1938 to accompany the novels to be reprinted in Scribner's Virginia Edition, and it was her wish that those prefaces be collected into a single volume (which she intended to title *The Anatomy of a Novel*). Even though Glasgow had long planned to write her autobiography, she delayed that effort to complete the prefaces in *A Certain Measure*. She realized that her final successes would have to come through acceptance by the male literary lions.

Drafts of both Glasgow's prefaces and her later autobiography show the effects of her practiced "humility," just as they reveal her consciousness of having to work hard to succeed as a writer. If one were a woman writer, merely writing well would never suffice. In a draft of *The Woman Within*, for example, she had said candidly,

Mercifully, as they say, I was spared the gift of prescience. I could not look ahead and see the thirty years of writing without recognition. I could not see the recognition that came grudgingly and came too late when it came at all. I could not feel the loneliness in which I stood and watched the ceaseless exaltation of the average.[24]

Reading *A Certain Measure* upon its publication in 1943, however, one would never guess that Glasgow was angry over lack of attention. The primary impression of the prefaces was rather that of Glasgow as a dedicated novelist, working against the stifling conventions of literary art. "I was, in my humble place and way, beginning a solitary revolt against the formal, the false, and affected, the sentimental, and the pretentious, in Southern writing. I had no guide. I was, so far as I was then aware, alone in my rejection of a prescribed and moribund convention of letters. But I felt, 'Life is not like this.' I thought, 'Why must novels be false to experience?'"[25]

Discounting the humility here, the reader can see that Glasgow is stressing the use of real experience; by implication, her female experience would then be a legitimate source of knowledge and character. She seldom mentions that identity directly but *A Certain Measure* is filled with declarations of her desire to write: "I had always wished to be a novelist. I cannot remember that I had ever wished to be anything else" (54). And the book has many explanations of her own process of becom-

ing a writer: "I wrote solely in obedience to some inward pressure. . . .
I have written chiefly because, though I have often dreaded the necessity, I have found it more painful, in the end, not to write" (68). She
describes movingly her conviction that, after finishing a novel, she "had
grown in the writing" (102) just as she reaffirms that "all creative writing
is an extension of personality," "a continual becoming" (112, 111).
Glasgow comes closer and closer to the themes of *The Woman Within* as
she insists that personality must fuse with the writer's art, the "brush-
strokes": the writer can write best about personal knowledge; the greatest novels depend upon "power, passion, pity, ecstasy and anguish,
hope and despair" (148). Their themes grow from the "transfigured experience" of real life (196).

Because Glasgow had come to place such emphasis on reality and
experience, her fiction frequently dealt with women characters and
themes that their lives could illustrate. *Barren Ground* interested Glasgow at least partly because she could turn the trite literary convention
of woman betrayed into a novel of woman betrayed as victor; as she said
gleefully about Dorinda, "She would triumph through that deep instinct for survival. . . . She would be hardened by adversity, but hard
things, as she said, are the last to decay. And she would never lose her
inner fidelity, that vital affirmation of life, 'I think, I feel, I am'" (160).
Glasgow had written many years before she was able to define the importance of "transfigured experience" and to acknowledge that it was
often transfigured female experience that most involved her.

She had early sensed that Southern fancy was inaccurate; she had also
rejected conventional literary realism, driving instead toward depictions
of characters' inner reality. Although she comments on method and technique throughout *A Certain Measure*, the focus of her attention as novelist is character, a means of using her own involvement as human
being. The evolution of Glasgow's skill in her best later fiction clearly
stems from her own deeply felt experiences. Perhaps because her pro-
duction was comparatively steady and her personal life relatively private, the correlation between life and work has sometimes gone un-
noticed; she herself speaks often of that correlation, however, as in this
1902 letter to Walter Hines Page:

> You have made it all seem worth while, somehow—the work and
> the struggle, and the going on to an aim, which in itself can be but
> a little thing. But in the highest sense you have given me encourage-
> ment, even when you did not dream that I needed it, when you did
> not know how bitterly I wanted to throw it away—and life with it.

The years have brought a good many things to me, but they have
taken them all away again except my work. Whether my own life
goes into my books I do not know, but such as are in me I must
write, and it will always be the quiet, happy souls who will turn out
the popular romances, and we others, who have never been able to
forget our Gethsemane and our cross, will continue to inflict upon
our publishers the books that go down into the heart of things and
appeal to those few that have been there before us. (*L.*, 40–41)

What is particularly interesting in Glasgow's development is that it is
often her experiences with women and women's needs that prompt her
best work: the deaths of Cary and her mother, for example, gave her the
impetus for *Virginia*. And one can sense her satisfaction when she
writes in a different tone of female friendships as she pictured them in
They Stooped to Folly:

It is seldom in modern fiction that a friendship between two
women, especially a pure and unselfish friendship . . . has assumed
a prominent place. Although such an association appears to be not
uncommon in life, the novelist, since he is usually a man, has found
the relationship to be deficient alike in the excitement of sex and the
masculine drama of action. But more and more, in the modern
world, women are coming to understand their interdependence as
human beings; and without an example of this, a picture of our
time that denied the place and the permanence of any such friendship would be wanting in complete veracity. (245)

Despite her apologetic tone, Glasgow succeeded in drawing believable
characters in believable situations. That those characters were, in the
course of her writing career, more and more often women proves how
intimate the relationship between life and art must be.

Because of Glasgow's intense personal involvement in the process of
her art, her autobiography *The Woman Within* complements *A Certain
Measure*. The two accounts—one ostensibly of her life and the other of
her art—dovetail into a collage that gives us at least a partial view of
Ellen Glasgow, woman writer:

If I have missed many of the external rewards of success, I have
never lost the outward peace and the inward compensation that
come from doing the work one wishes to do in the solitary way in
which one wishes to do it . . . I wanted "a room of my own,"

and it was granted me. I wanted a pursuit that I might follow
with interest between the cradle and the grave, and that, too, was
allowed. (*CM*, 178)

For today's reader, that last verb *allowed* echoes through any self-
congratulation. Society, family, friends, lovers—Glasgow gives us the
image of the frail Southern daughter holding staunchly to her ambition
in the midst of countless pressures to conform.

"More than thirty years ago, I began my literary work as a rebel
against conventions. I am still a rebel, but the conventions are different," Glasgow wrote in an unpublished essay.[26] There seems little
reason to wonder about the consistently defensive tone that colors her
autobiographical writing; indeed, the only wonder is that her defensive-
ness appears as infrequently as it does. Tillie Olsen's *Silences* speaks in
rich detail of the difficulties of being a writer in a relatively hostile culture,[27] but the life and work of Ellen Glasgow create a paradigm of those
difficulties. What Glasgow accomplished in spite of her milieu is worth
celebration today.

CHAPTER 2

The Early Novels

"In that far republic of the spirit I ranged, free and wild, and a rebel."[1] Glasgow's recollection of her adolescence—marked by disagreements with her father and family over philosophical views and behavior—may be over romanticized. It is one thing to be intellectually independent, as her forays into Darwin, Spencer, Mill, and others suggest. It is another to feel isolated, and betrayed in that isolation. When she describes the periods of bewildered loneliness and anger during her childhood, Glasgow shields no one.

> And indeed through all my future life, I shrank from my father's presence; and only one of my elder sisters ever won my reluctant confidence. At the time, angry, defiant, utterly unsubdued by pleadings and rebukes, I told myself, obstinately, that if they cared nothing for my feelings, I would care nothing for theirs. For weeks I hated them all. I hated the things they believed in, the things they so innocently and charmingly pretended. I hated the sanctimonious piety that let people hurt helpless creatures. (71)

Not only were Glasgow's interests and temperament consistently at odds with her family's expectations, but they led her to leave the religion of her ancestry. They also led her to defenses of other people and animals that she felt needed protecting.

> Rage convulsed me, the red rage that must have swept up from the jungles . . . it contained every anger, every revolt I had ever felt in my life—the way I felt when I saw the black dog hunted, the way I felt when I watched old Uncle Henry taken away to the almshouse, the way I felt whenever I had seen people or animals hurt for the pleasure or profit of others. (70)

In each of these passages from *The Woman Within*, Glasgow suggests the affinity between the helpless human and animals. Her continuous work for the Society for the Prevention of Cruelty to Animals is as much an outgrowth of those early sentiments as was her fiction, with its sympathy for the protected but powerless female.

J. R. Raper's masterful studies of Glasgow's education and maturation (the 1971 *Without Shelter: The Early Career of Ellen Glasgow* and the 1980 *From the Sunken Garden: The Fiction of Ellen Glasgow, 1916–1945*) include exhaustive accounts of the reading she began in her adolescence. His description is enlightening. The only reservation one might have about Raper's thesis is that he sometimes discounts the human needs which forced Glasgow into her study of economics, science, and philosophy. Glasgow's intellectual adventures were a refuge in part from her disordered world, a world which was chaotic and disappointing beneath its veneer of reason. To come to terms with the discrepancies between what society maintained and what it actually permitted (whether in double sexual standards or religious beliefs), Glasgow searched in many places. She was attracted by the study of important writers and thinkers. She enjoyed challenging people's concepts about which books a young Southern woman should be reading. She was also trying urgently to find answers for herself about nearly every conceivable problem—women's place in the world, love and marriage, religion, poverty and wealth, self-determination. And as Raper concludes,

> Ellen Glasgow . . . had to fight day by day for her freedom. She did not always succeed. If it seems paradoxical that her freedom depended on the authority of so long a list of Darwinists, one must be reminded of the awful pressure southern provincialism exerts to force the conformity of all southerners to its monolithic world view: to resist she needed every support she could reach.[2]

Once Glasgow began writing fiction in the 1890's, the pressures of her place as a privileged Southern woman became all too evident. Both the kinds of women characters she chose to write about and her treatment of them revealed the conflict between her personal ideal woman and that woman's place in her culture. Her ideal contradicted the feminine ideal of the traditional Virginia society in which she herself lived and wrote.

The ideal Southern woman—as Glasgow knew from her own family's attitudes—was to be deferential to the patriarch of the family or, in his absence, to any other male—uncle, brother, nephew. If she challenged that male direction, she was only acting whimsically and, as a deviant from reasonable behavior, she could then be scolded, cajoled, or humored. Any serious breach in conduct, however, that threatened family position or honor, or virginity, could mean ostracism. Anne Firor Scott concludes that the power of the proper image for a Southern lady was particularly strong and did in reality shape behavior. Of the South she writes,

> The social role of women was unusually confining there, and the sanctions used to enforce obedience peculiarly effective. One result was that southern women became in time a distinct type among American women. Another was that their efforts to free themselves were more complex than those of women elsewhere.[3]

Glasgow's early novels are filled with worn women whose lives have been poured on the altar of that obedience. Pale shadows like Mrs. Pendleton and Mrs. Carr, seemingly blessed in marriage and progeny, are in Glasgow's presentation bereft of any personal spirit. She describes such women in her 1898 novel, *Phases of an Inferior Planet*, as

> that numerous army of women who fulfil life as they fulfil an appointment at the dentist's—with a desperate sense of duty and shaken nerves. . . . The saints of old, who were sanctified by fire and sword, might well shrink from the martyrdom sustained, smiling, by many who have endured the rack of daily despair.[4]

The chief role of these sanctified wives and mothers in Glasgow's early fiction is to provide stability for their less complacent daughters, the willful "modern" women—Mariana Musin, Rachel Gavin, Virginia Pendleton, Gabriella Carr. Mothers give love and fearful wisdom; their advice conveys vividly the social and familial expectations for the heroines. But Glasgow never presents these mature women as role models, they serve rather as specters of the predictable female. By slanting her readers against the very women characters who should be beloved and respected, and by allowing these women to glimpse the promise lost for themselves, Glasgow establishes sympathy with those female characters who are trying to exist outside of tradition—she in effect justifies the rebellious daughters.

At the heart of the many conventions affecting women's lives, Glasgow suggests through her fiction, lies the myth of the primacy of romantic love. Once a woman had a man to love—a man who loved, honored, and cared for her—her life was complete. Such a relationship would provide both vocation and avocation, physical passion and intellectual stimulus. In the case of Mariana Musin, the aspiring singer in *Phases of an Inferior Planet* who lived alone in New York, marriage to the young scholar Anthony Algarcife meant accepting the fallacy that "love is a self-sustaining force, independent of material conditions. 'So long as we love each other,' Mariana declared, 'nothing matters'" (112). With the physical possession that Anthony brings to the marriage, Mariana's bondage is complete:

> "If you knew how I love you," he said slowly—"if you only knew! There is no happiness in it; it is agony. I am afraid—afraid for the first time in my life—afraid of losing you."
> "You shall never lose me."
> "It is a horrible thing, this fear—this fear for something outside of yourself!" He spoke with a sudden, half-fierce possession. "You are mine," he said, "and you love me!" (99)

The impossible weight resting on a fragile relationship was doomed to crush it, and Glasgow used and reused the romantic formula precisely to show that predictable outcome. Already in the 1898 *Planet*, Mariana's conflict is partly self-inflicted. It lies between her love for Anthony, imaged as her satisfaction in the role of wife, and her ambition to sing ("My God! I would give ten years of my life for that—to sing with Alvary," 71). Glasgow defines the conflict clearly as she tells the reader that "Anthony's objection seemed to lie like a drawn sword between her and her art."

> It was not that her devotion to art had cooled since her marriage, but that something was forever preventing the expression of it. That Anthony regarded it as one of the trivialities of life, she saw clearly, and there was an aggrieved note in her regret. To her, in whom the artistic instinct was bone of her bone and blood of her blood, the sacrifice of a professional career was less slight than Algarcife believed, and in the depths of her heart there still lurked the hope that in time Anthony's impassioned opposition to a stage life would wear itself out. (122)

In the words of her voice instructor, the wise Signor Morani, Mariana would keep her equilibrium as artist and person only if she would remember "that you are an artist first, and a wife and mother afterwards" (123). Few people in Mariana's culture—or Glasgow's—would have shared that belief.

The false assurances of the protected life of a beloved woman combined with the scarcity of career options for late-Victorian women gave Glasgow—and countless other women writers contemporary with her—a set of traditional plots and reader expectations, but Glasgow worked from the beginning of her career to avoid those expectations. Her first novels are flawed at least partly because she tried so hard to avoid the stock-in-trades: the happy heroine who does marry, becomes disillusioned, but endures; or the fallen heroine, the bright, virtuous woman who is made to pay for her pride or ambition or misplaced passion. (That woman's punishment is, predictably, the loss of her lover.) In trying to avoid happy endings, Glasgow was often guilty of deus-ex-machina deaths or coincidences; readers, however, forgave her these contrivances because, even from the start of her career, her characters were effective.

Many of Glasgow's ingénue heroines were prototypes of the young Ellen—audacious, winsome, free-thinking, distinctive without being beautiful, passionate, defiant, and ambitious. From Rachel Gavin to Betty Ambler to Dorinda Oakley, these heroines are different from the other women of the novels (and Glasgow used many foil characters to point up those differences). Generous to a fault, Glasgow's young heroines either love too well or refuse to love; they may not be intellectual but they are at least questioning. They want to know where they are headed and why; indeed, their personal catastrophes often occur because of this questioning, this spirit that keeps them from accepting the convention of "woman's place."

Even though her interest in these ambitious and unconventional heroines was evident, the structures of Glasgow's first novels—and their titles—suggest that she was more comfortable with male protagonists. The heroine in an early book often assumes a secondary place as the hero's romantic partner. The plot of the novel follows the hero—Michael Akershem in *The Descendant* is leading a maverick life as an educated liberal, despite his illegitimate birth; Anthony Algarcife moves from avowed agnosticism early in *Phases of an Inferior Planet* to the later hypocritical vocation of Episcopalian priest; Nicholas Burr, the hero of Glasgow's third novel, *The Voice of the People*, brings himself Alger-like to martyrdom. Glasgow's heroes often fit Elaine Showalter's description of the Victorian hero:

> The model heroes are the product of female fantasies that are much more concerned with power and authority than with romance. Many of these heroes are extremely aggressive in bourgeois economic terms. They are successful; they live out the fairy tale of

Victorian upward mobility with the single-minded energy that characterized their female creators.[5]

Glasgow may have felt that readers would be interested primarily in the outcomes of male characters' lives. They could succeed or fail on both economic or personal terms. In contrast, what could happen to a heroine that would keep a reader reading? Heroines were either married or unmarried: even though a woman might be a professional, society saw any occupation as only secondary to the role every woman was to assume—that of wife. Because the happiness of the heroine depended on the quality and circumstances of the man she loved, the hero was of necessity crucial to the novel. That Glasgow's early novels all focused on dominant women characters whose importance diminished during the second half of the novel might suggest her feeling that readers would be less interested in the outcome of female personae.

These early novels also testify to Glasgow's own rearing in the belief that certain kinds of activities are more valuable than others, just as certain kinds of knowledge—philosophy, science, history—are also more valuable. Just as it took her twenty years to be comfortable writing about a female protagonist, so it took many years before she would write about the joy of gardening. Characters in her early novels don't garden or cook, though Glasgow's notebooks are full of recipes; they discuss free will, Malthus, and John Stuart Mill. When critics guessed that Glasgow's anonymous first novel, *The Descendant*, had been written by Harold Frederic, author of *The Damnation of Theron Ware*, Glasgow was delighted. She may have been a woman writer, but during the 1890's she was a woman writer trying desperately to pretend that she was, in fact, a liberal, well-educated man. For her as for most of her readers, the proper focus of serious literature was man; its proper subjects were the great moral issues.

Glasgow's first novel, *The Descendant*, in some ways expresses what come to be the author's mature beliefs about people. She draws characters which represent two of her favorite situations: boy making good despite circumstances of birth; girl making good in nonconventional ways. Michael Akershem's academic ability gives him a means out of his life of poverty. Before he is twenty-six, he climbs to the editorship of the sensational *Iconoclast* in New York. Feared by conservatives, he becomes known as the antidemocracy, anti-God, antimarriage spokesman of the most liberal coterie in the city. His attraction for Rachel Gavin, an aspiring and talented painter, stems at least partly from her independence: "Miss Gavin was emancipated, or believed herself to be, which amounts to the same thing."[6]

Unfortunately for both Rachel and Michael—but most of all for their relationship—Rachel thinks she has found a superior person in Michael. In her worship of him, she gives up the very ambition that he so admires. The scene of her capitulation is pointed:

> She was conscious of having been called away from her self-absorption, of having been betrayed into reverencing a man, a man who was leader and pioneer of what the world called a non-moral element, but a man who was strong enough to stand fearlessly alone—ah, that was a man! (82)

Glasgow juxtaposes this careful description with the scene immediately following, when Rachel moves to the covered canvas of her unfinished masterpiece, the portrait of a woman,

> a half-finished Magdalen, a rough peasant Magdalen, with traces of sinful passion and sinful suffering upon her face. A woman who, having been dragged through the mire and slime, forever carried the stains upon her broken body. It was a great work, as she had said, a work which showed the hand of genius, a hand whose strokes are powerful and falter not.
> She let the curtain fall and turned away.
> "How strong he is," she said. (82)

The impact of the masculine pronoun *he*, after the reader has been so thoroughly convinced of the strength of both Rachel and the Magdalen, sets the tone for the remaining two hundred pages of the book. Rachel's trust is misplaced: she abandons her own important work to love Michael, and loses her social and self-acceptance in that loving, only to have him discard her for her very self-abnegation ("In his future Rachel had no place. Now he wanted . . . the one thing she had not . . . the honor of good men and good women. . . . A pure woman would have spurned passion for the sake of principle!" 192). Even though Michael is later to realize "the wealth of her nature, the immensity of the love with which she had loved him," that realization does little to counter the irony of Glasgow's theme (282). She announces that theme early in the novel, describing Rachel: "She had not learned that the enemy of woman is neither God, man, nor devil, but her own heart" (83).

Rachel's lack of any genuine sense of worth combines with those "traditional" expectations of women's lives, forcing the woman who tries to find new roles into precarious situations. Rachel meets this undermining in the prayer scene, when she asks for the strength and concentration to finish her work; but then she willingly abandons that work to go with Michael. It is only eight years later—after their affair has ended and Michael has been imprisoned for manslaughter (an unfortunate plot contrivance)—that Rachel finishes the much-acclaimed painting. That her own suffering has mirrored Magdalen's has given her the capacity to excel in her art.

Written in 1897, *The Descendant* is a predictable mixture of sentiment and effectiveness, marred with the rhetoric of much philosophical discussion at the *Iconoclast* offices and an overreliance on deus ex machina. It does, however, show Glasgow's early conviction that women—and their inherited attitudes and traditions—create their own tragedies. *The Descendant* is a surprisingly mature statement about the fragility of human passion, and a surprisingly contemporary indictment of social attitudes toward women.

One year later Glasgow's second novel, *Phases of an Inferior Planet*, continues these themes, but the indictment here falls more directly on conventional male attitudes as being responsible for women's difficulties in achieving fulfillment. Glasgow was still burdened with her interest in economics and skepticism, and this novel is almost a casebook for the stances she is both testifying to and breaking with. The novel opens with the story of Mariana Musin, "graceful and feminine and fragile." Subtle enough not to offend, Mariana has yet managed to get her family to finance her studying voice, and living independently, in New York City. She seems to be strong-willed; however, she is really a mixture of confidence and timidity. Chameleon-like, she adapts to cultural expectations. Like many less independent women, Mariana also places paramount value on love; Glasgow tells us that, even though Mariana seemed to be ambitious, "Her longings for fame and for love were so closely interwoven that even in her own mind it was impossible to disassociate them" (22). Because she arrives in New York "famished for romance," the sudden engagement and marriage to Anthony is predictable.

Glasgow barbs her tragedy of the death of the great passion with the summary that both lovers "accepted in its entirety the fallacy that love is a self-sustaining force, independent of material conditions." Poverty, dissatisfaction, the frustration of both people's careers—the novel presents scene after scene that explains the disappointments inherent in such unrealistic expectations.

To complicate the emotional situation, Mariana has given up her music, her ambition to be an opera singer. With her marriage, as Glasgow describes it,

> She threw herself into the worship of him with absolute disregard of all retarding interests. When he was near, she lavished demonstrations upon him; when he was away, she sat with folded hands and dreamed day dreams. She had given up her music, and she even went so far as to declare that she would give up her acquaintances, that they might be sufficient unto each other. For his sake she discussed theories which she did not understand, and accepted doctrines of which she had once been intolerant. That emotional energy which had led her imagination into devious ways had at last, she told herself, found its appropriate channel. (102)

Glasgow's terminology here—"she told herself," "devious ways," "appropriate channel"—signals to the reader that Mariana's "emotional energy" is viewed not as a strength but as a detriment, even an embarrassment. Passion, energy, the reliance on intuition—these feminine qualities are the subject of discussion throughout the novel and, although Mariana defends her right to them, she is purposely whimsical and unconvincing in her arguments. It is all too clear that she has been trained to think herself, and her talent, inferior; that she has little sense of her own selfhood. The issues are finally far beyond a woman's talent for opera or hat-trimming, however, as Glasgow suggests in several places that a central issue is Anthony's ownership of Mariana: "He possessed her, this was sufficient. She was to be his forever, come what would" (306).

Glasgow pictures Anthony's love for Mariana as an extension of that for his mother; he finds his love for her deepest after their child, Isolt, is born and dies. Mariana as mother (the Mariolatry suggested in her name leads directly to this impression) is his deity, and the parallels with the saintly Mrs. Ryder later in the novel strengthen that suggestion. With childlike possessiveness, Anthony demands all: Mariana's physical debilitation illustrates that demand. When she remarries, he is so incensed at her defilement that he refuses to speak to her. No mother—at least not any mother of his—would behave in such a way. The concept of virtue as physical purity appears here; had Mariana not had sex with another man, then she would have been, still, his. He appears to forget that he could have prevented her divorce and re-marriage.

That Glasgow is trying to set the Mariana-Anthony story in a larger context is partly responsible for the clumsy denouement, and for the equally clumsy title. The most naturalistic of her books, *Phases of an Inferior Planet* proposes that passion is inexplicable, that love is fated, and that fate also controls the outcome of those who people this planet. The susceptibility to passion, the realization of instinct, *is* the human quality, Glasgow states. It is only when Anthony denounces his love for Mariana that he becomes alien:

> As he passed among men and women he was aware of a strange aloofness, as if the links connecting him with his kind had snapped asunder; and he felt that he might have been the being of another planet to whom earthly passions and fulfilments bore no palpable relation, but were to be considered with cosmic composure. (183)

Only in Anthony's terms would earth be "inferior," however, for Glasgow, like Mariana, was sympathetic toward passion. The epigraphs to parts one and two extend the comparison. Part one has as epigraph, "Some turned to folly and the sweet works of the flesh," which suggests the pleasure of passion, whereas part two's preface suggests only the dissension Anthony himself creates: "And not even here do all agree—no, not any one with himself." The purely intellectual adjustment which has become Anthony's way of existing in the latter part of the novel is sterile. Glasgow presents, as alternative, the intuitive under-standing that exists between Mariana and Mrs. Ryder, "in whom feeling is predominant over thought, and to whom life represents a rhythmic series of emotions rather than waves of mental evolution" (226).

United as the women are in the love of the Ryder child, they have no need for verbal strategies, lies, hypocrisy. Their behavior differs from Anthony's. He is so confused that he duels, in print, with his former self. Algarcife is both the agnostic who wrote essays for the *Scientific Weekly* ten years before, and the now celibate priest who "answers" those essays. He is outside humanity, condemning even while he serves as model for his parishioners. That Mariana would rather die than de-stroy Anthony's image for those deluded parishioners, and for himself, is the tragic irony of the novel. Once they are reunited, Mariana senses that their elopement will be disastrous. She questions her own ability to stand poverty, but the chief problem, as she seems to sense, will be Anthony's changed self-image. Even in her death she thinks primarily of him. And in his ability to carry on, despite his genuine grief, Glasgow shows the falsity of his virtue. As she was to say much later, "Self-sacrifice may ruin lives as utterly as selfishness." [7]

With *The Voice of the People* in 1900, Glasgow finds her Southern subject and setting, but the characters of this novel lack the tone of reality evident in her first books. The seven-year-old heroine sounds like a Shirley Temple portrait; and the poor young hero, Nicholas Burr, is introduced in an incredibly maudlin scene:

> Then, as he caught sight of a smaller red head beneath Burr's arm, he added: "You've a right-hand man coming on, I see. What's your name, my boy?"
>
> The boy squirmed on his bare, brown feet and wriggled his head from beneath his father's arm. He did not answer, but he turned his bright eyes on the judge and flushed through all the freckles of his ugly little face.
>
> "Nick—that is, Nicholas, sir," replied the elder Burr with an apologetic cough. "Yes, sir, he's leetle, but he's plum full of grit. He can beat any nigger I ever seed at the plough. He'd out-plough me if he war a head taller." . . .
>
> "Oh, he'll be a man soon enough," added the judge, his gaze passing over the large, red head to rest upon the small one, "and a farmer like his father before him, I suppose."
>
> He was turning away when the child's voice checked him, and he paused.
>
> "I—I'd ruther be a judge," said the boy. [8]

As in her earlier novels, Glasgow gives the story to Nicholas, partly because his story has some conventional appeal, even though her interest in Eugenia Battle is keen. The childhood friendship between the wealthy Eugenia and the poor Nicholas and their brief engagement midway through the book bring the story lines together, but once Eugenia marries a more suitable man, Glasgow can include her only when her husband and Nicholas become political rivals. What drama exists lies in Eugenia's divided loyalty, but that is faint compared with Nicholas' idealistic career choices, which lead finally to his death. The reader is interested in Eugenia as the girl who would not accept society's pronouncements, who *would* love Nicholas despite his social position, but that attention falters later in the novel when Eugenia becomes a one-dimensional helpmeet to her husband.

Writing thirty-five years later in the preface to the Virginia Edition, Glasgow describes Nicholas as yet another of "the disinherited of society," the type of character she worked with consistently. She also saw him then as "the civilized offspring of the primitive protagonist in *The Descendant*" (x, ix). Burr aims for a career in law and politics, and for Eugenia as his bride. Slandered to save her brother's reputation, Burr gives up the latter ambition but manages to rise to the governorship of Virginia. The plot holds more interest than such a summary suggests because Glasgow points throughout to the difference between male and female choice. As Judge Battle had answered an irate mother when she disapproved of Burr's being educated with her son (she saying, "It is a folly to educate a person above his station"): "Men make their stations, madam" (83). Men can choose to rise, to determine their own direction; women, even women as independent as Eugenia, are as hobbled in their choices as they are in their garments. Glasgow sets a miniature of that hobbling just after Eugenia agrees to wait for Burr, foreshadowing the conflicts even the strongest woman meets when she opposes convention:

> At the fence she gave him the bunch and swung herself lightly over the sunken rails. It did not occur to him to assist her; she had always been as good as he at vaulting bars. Now her long skirts retarded her, and she laughed as she came quickly to the ground on the opposite side.
> "The best prisons men ever invented are women's skirts," she said. "Our wings are clipped while we wear them."
> "It is hard," he returned as he recalled her schoolgirl feats. "You were such a jumper."
> "Those halcyon days are done," she sighed. "I can never stray beyond my sphere again." (167)

Social pressure forces Eugenia to break her promise to wait for Burr and to marry another man. Sixteen years later, after Burr's death at the hands of a lynch mob, Glasgow pictures her as firmly caught within that sphere: "She was not thinking; she was merely resting from emotion, as she would rest for all the quiet remainder of her days . . . somewhere there was, there would be always, she knew, a lost ecstasy" (324–25).

Glasgow's interest in the self-made hero, which continues for the next twenty years, may be simply a consistent reliance on the popular American Alger theme, but it might also suggest the character of the mysterious Gerald B., the married man she loved from approximately

1900 to the end of the affair, or his death, in 1906.[9] According to her account in *The Woman Within*, Gerald B. was the first man she had loved "with her whole being" (153). "Looking back, over the flat surface of experience, the whole occurrence appears incredibly wild and romantic. It does not belong to life; yet it remains, after all the years between, intensely alive. It is the one thing that has not passed; for not ever again, in the future, could I see my life closing as if it had not once bloomed and opened wide to the light" (155). As Glasgow commented on those years, "For the next seven years I lived in an arrested pause between dreaming and waking. All reality was poured into a solitary brooding power, a solitary emotion" (160).

Because the romance continued these six or seven years, replete with great secrecy and, one supposes, great guilt on Glasgow's part, her fiction during these years would probably have been colored by the experience. If Glasgow's reminiscence is to be believed, she endured the affair hoping that someday Gerald B. and she would marry; the character of the loving, waiting woman thus represents Glasgow herself during these years. Eugenia Battle promises to wait for Burr in *The Voice of the People*; Betty Ambler waits through the anguish of the Civil War and is finally rewarded with Dan Lightfoot's return in *The Battle-Ground*; and in 1904, in *The Deliverance*, a bitter man is redeemed by the love of a returning heroine (who then waits for him in turn). In both *The Battle-Ground* and *The Deliverance*, Glasgow creates the happy ending she had avoided in her first three novels, the happy ending which results only because of the wise persistence of the loving heroine.

For all their ostensible independence, however, Eugenia, Betty, and Maria Fletcher of *The Deliverance* are all single-minded; each lives only to capture her husband. Betty Ambler, like Eugenia, has loved her husband-to-be since they were children. When Dan appears on a deserted road and taunts her that he is her Prince, she shares with him her "girlish visions" of the man she will marry:

> He will be a man . . . with a faith to fight for—to live for—to make him noble. He may be a beggar by the roadside, but he will be a beggar with dreams. He will be forever travelling to some great end—some clear purpose.[10]

Betty's life is built around that dream, and one could make the extension to the kind of men Glasgow herself admired—men of purpose, idealism, dedication.

Whereas attention in *The Battle-Ground* is consistently usurped by Betty Ambler, Glasgow works hard in *The Deliverance* to keep Christopher Blake, another alien superhero, central. In this novel Glasgow has reversed the strengths of hero and heroine. Blake is no ascetic; his life is ruled not by a denial of emotion but by an exploitation of the strongest of feelings, that of hate. Blake exists only to avenge his family's honor against Bill Fletcher, who has stolen the Blake land and home. Ironically, Blake's salvation as a human being occurs through his love for Maria Fletcher, the granddaughter of his enemy, whose balanced view of life and search for virtue set the moralistic tone of the book. Maria's knowledge is the product of both education and experience; her strength enables her to redeem Blake both physically and emotionally.

The reversal in roles here continues what was to be Glasgow's intentional tampering with reader expectation. The practical wisdom of life usually came from the mature, well-traveled hero; instead of hero, Glasgow gives us Maria. It is Christopher who lives caught in a confining environment, depressed by work, duty, resentment. Instead of a virginal daughter, Glasgow gives us the virginal son. Regardless of the shift in roles, the traditional element in the plot remains the romance— the great passion existing between Christopher and Maria, to which the title refers.

That Glasgow identified with Maria—romantic or no—was again clear. She was not only a woman, enabling Glasgow to continue her portrayal of strong females; she was also a maverick. Maria defied the ignoble Fletcher ancestry (whereas her brother Will is one of Glasgow's most craven characters). Fascinated by people who managed to escape the claims of inherited traits, Glasgow recalled,

> In the character of Maria Fletcher, I have dealt again with the higher offspring of a lower form. Just as Nicholas Burr in *The Voice of the People* was a superior variation from an inferior type, so Maria exemplified a woman's upspringing from poorer stock, and her development away from the family pattern.[11]

Aligning Maria with an important source of wisdom, the venerable Uncle Tucker, strengthens Maria's position—though one could scarcely doubt her moral superiority when she instructs Christopher:

> "You remembered them even while you were away?"
> "Why not?" she asked. "It is not the moving about, the strange

places one sees, nor the people one meets, that really count in life, you know."

"What is it?" he questioned abruptly.

She hesitated, as if trying to put her thoughts more clearly into words.

"I think it is the things one learns," she said; "the places in which we take root and grow, and the people who teach us what is really worth while; patience, and charity, and the beauty there is in the simplest and most common lives when they are lived close to nature."

"In driving the plough or in picking the suckers from a tobacco plant," he added scornfully.

"In those things, yes; and in any life that is good, and true, and natural." (256–57)

Christopher remains the romantic: "I want the excitement that makes one's blood run like wine. . . . War, and fame, and love" (257). In his inability to call things by accurate names, Christopher loses further credibility and joins the number of Glasgow's heroes who continually fail to face reality. One is reminded of Glasgow's definition of herself as "verist," not romancer or realist. Her 1938 preface to *The Battle-Ground* also remarks that the novel "is not a romance"; "it is, nevertheless, the work of romantic youth. The person who conceived it is nowadays a dead person" (x). In the corresponding preface to *The Deliverance*, she speaks of Maria's love being able to change Christopher's character, and admits,

> Had I written this book at the present time, it is probable that I should have subdued the romantic note to an ending of stark tragedy. . . . I have doubted, in later years, whether any love, however exalted, could have conquered the triumphant hatred in Christopher's heart and mind. (xviii)

Written during the joy of her romance with Gerald B., these two novels are the only early books in which Glasgow's heroine and hero are united at the novel's end, apparently to share the future. As *The Battle-Ground* ends, Betty says, "'We will begin again . . . and this time, my dear, we will begin together'" (387); *The Deliverance* closes with Maria coming to welcome Christopher "across the sunbeams" (398). Of this period in Glasgow's own life, little remains except her account in her autobiography. As she wrote to her literary executors, only letters from 1916 and after remain; none exists from the 1900–1906 period. In a 1944 letter, she explained,

> Many of my earlier letters, especially the more personal letters, I myself burned, when I left home, as I thought forever, on a long wandering, in search of place, after the heartbreaking loss of my beloved sister, Cary McCormack [1911].[12]

In a letter dated 1945 she phrased the same information somewhat differently, "At other times, in a desperate resolve to escape from the tragedy of the past, I destroyed all the letters I had kept by me for years. Those that I did not destroy meant less to me and awoke no heartbreaking memories."[13]

Fragmentary as accounts of Glasgow's first romance remain, *The Battle-Ground* and *The Deliverance* exist as tributes to the years when she believed, however briefly, in the romantic myths of her girlhood. It would be later that Glasgow would adopt the ironic mode so often associated with her fiction—later, once this great love was finished and she was left quoting Oscar Wilde, "The worst of romances is that they leave one so unromantic."[14]

CHAPTER 3

The Years of Loss

In countless letters and autobiographical writings, Glasgow describes her grief at the loss of Gerald B. The anguish she experienced for the several years after 1905 is unquestionable; she recalls in *The Woman Within* "a period of death-in-life" during which she had little feeling and could, in fact, taste nothing.[1] Letters written later recall the same despair, as when she consoles Mary Johnston, whose health had been very bad at one time:

> A year ago I passed through exactly the same awakening of myself, though from different causes. Mine was not physical, but spiritual—mental—what you will! For a year I was so dead that I couldn't feel even when I was hurt because of some curious emotional anaesthesia, and, like you, I had to fight—fight, a sleepless battle night and day, not for my reason but for my very soul. Then at the end of a year—at Murren last summer I came out triumphant, and for three whole months it was as if I walked on light, not air. . . . We suffered in different ways, but we both suffered to the death—each of us saw at the end of her road the mouth of hell—and each of us turned and struggled back to life—you along your steep path and I along mine. (*L.*, 55–56)

Glasgow's life was marred with the losses of family members and friends, and her susceptibility to depression because of these losses is easily documented. She herself described her severe depression after both her mother's death in 1893 and her sister Cary's in 1911; the reader can assume a similar condition following the end of her affair. The disorientation which followed her mother's death caused much physical illness (including the beginning of her deafness) as well as an apathy which led to her destroying four hundred pages of an early version of *The Descendant*. After this period, Glasgow did not write again for several years. She speaks in her autobiography of "my mother's slow martyrdom, which had drained the joy from my veins" (113). Similarly, after Cary's death, Glasgow left home ("as I thought forever, on a long wandering, in search of place") so as to break all ties with her remaining family. The poignancy of Betty Ambler's grief for her lost sister in *The Battle-Ground*, a book dedicated to Glasgow's mother, suggests the immensity of her grieving for that woman: "I have missed Virginia so— never a day passes that I do not see her coming through the rooms and hear her laugh—such a baby laugh, do you remember. . . . I have almost died with wanting her again" (320).

Glasgow's fiction also gives us a glimpse of her state of mind after the end of Gerald B.'s romance. In her later novel, *In This Our Life*, the heroine finally accepts her husband's death as a release from all expectation:

> Now, at last, it was really over; it was fulfilled and finished forever. Now she would never look for him, never expect him to return, never again be tormented by those frail and fleeting resemblances in the street. Now, at last, she was safe from him; she had escaped into finality. Her identity was secure, was protected by death, by utter finality. She was secure against any return, and secure, too, against the scorching (burning) jealousy to which she had never given a name.[2]

Again, Glasgow writes powerfully of this mixture of sentiments, even jealousy, because she would have known them all during the romance as she describes it. And there remain some 1909 letters to her close friend, Elizabeth Patterson, in which she speaks of the summer of 1906, "I don't believe anybody else in the world would have been—or could have been—as understanding as you were then." "I wrote Cary a few days ago that no one had ever been dearer to me than you were in England. I love you more and more whenever I look back on it."[3]

Although she was to become engaged from 1907 to 1910 to the Reverend Frank Paradise, Glasgow seemed to have reached the decision that the best protection against hurt was noninvolvement. "Peace dwells in impersonality alone. Beyond the personal," she writes in notes to a late novel.[4] She was evidently turning once again to philosophy to reconstruct a world which was not dependent on romance or idealization, as is evident in her 1906 novel, *The Wheel of Life*. These are the years Frederick P. W. McDowell calls her "mystical phase," a period in which she turned to moral and philosophical idealism to give her a sense of stability. The novel that resulted tried to create happiness from renunciation; at its best it was ineffectual.[5]

The Wheel of Life mates a beautiful otherworldly poetess with an understanding older lover, whose wife has finally died after years of drug abuse and scandal. The romance of Laura and Roger constitutes the plot of the book, which, for all its happy ending, treats romantic conventions with refreshing irony. The chapter titles, for example, suggest that Glasgow is once again mocking prescriptive fiction:

Ch. 1   In Which the Romantic Hero Is Conspicuous by His Absence . . .

Ch. 6   Shows That Mr. Worldly-Wise-Man May Belong to Either Sex . . .

Ch. 10   Shows the Hero To Be Lacking in Heroic Qualities . . .

When Glasgow begins the novel by introducing Gerty and Percy Bridewell, partners of a brilliant but competitive society marriage, her emphasis is on the disillusionment in that marriage, especially for the bride Gerty.[6] Three eligible men are introduced as well, along with Gerty's poet friend, Laura Wilde, a clear prototype of Glasgow. There is, in fact, no hero: the man who at first appears to be one becomes in time the villain—Arnold Kemper, Laura's lover. Laura as heroine has for a tragic flaw the fact that she is a "romantic"; she has adopted the myth that women must give all to love, an attitude based on her mother's example. Her Uncle Percival's explanation of her parents' unhappiness is central to the author's viewpoint throughout the novel:

She wanted your father—every minute of him, every thought, every heart-beat. He couldn't give it to her, my dear. No man could. I tell you I have lived to a great age, and I have known great people, and I have never seen the man yet who could give a woman all the love she wanted. (25)

As the novel becomes the odyssey of Laura's pursuit of the idea of romance, personified in Kemper, Glasgow pits reality against illusion at every turn. Despite the wisdom of Uncle Percival and Roger Adams, Laura's true lover, she nearly follows illusion and marries Kemper. But it is her instinct for self-preservation, for freedom, that finally convinces her she must break the engagement: to be bound on the "wheel of life," as Gerty is, is the result of a tenuous marriage.

Glasgow structures the novel to parallel the stages of Laura's knowledge: Impulse (in which Laura yearns for love); Illusion (her love for Kemper); Disenchantment (the demise of the romance); and Reconciliation (reunion with self, not with Kemper). Significantly, when Laura is most bereft—of both love and illusion—Roger brings Gerty to her, instead of trying to comfort her himself. "Her heart is bleeding— it's a woman that she wants," he explains. And Glasgow reinforces the concept:

> Partly because she was a woman and partly because of her bitter triumphs, she had understood that the wisdom in love is the only wisdom which avails in the supreme agony of life. Neither philosophy nor religion mattered now, for presently she felt that her bosom was warm with tears, and when Laura lifted her head, the two women kissed in that intimate knowledge which is uttered without speech. (462)

This important scene occurs in "The Reconciliation." This title does not suggest a reconciliation between lovers but rather a rapprochement between the Laura who lived in illusion and the Laura who could face reality. Her way to that rapprochement—since it involved so many of the cultural and emotional patterns affecting women—was through her love for a woman. In *The Wheel of Life*, Glasgow shows that she has learned not only to attack romantic myths but also to provide alternatives for them. For in Laura's final conception of the word *love* ("all emotion is but the blind striving of love after the consciousness of itself," 474), she is able to relinquish language and to trust her feeling for people—Gerty, Roger, the poor to whom she devotes herself. The transcendence which Laura achieves (described in this novel as her resurrection brought about by the small blue flower) parallels the transfiguration Glasgow herself experienced just after her knowledge of the end of her affair.[7] The conclusion of her description of Laura's experience follows:

> Then as the minutes passed and her gaze did not waver from the blue petals filled with sunshine, she was aware gradually, as if between dream and waking, of a peculiar deepening of her mental vision, until there was revealed to her, while she looked, not only the outward semblance, but the essence of the flower which was its soul. And this essence of the flower came suddenly in contact with the dead soul within her bosom. . . . At this instant, by that divine miracle of resurrection she began to live anew—to live not her old life alone, but a life that was larger and fuller than the one which

had been hers. She began to live anew in herself as well as in the
sky and in humanity and in the songs of birds. (468–69)

Even though Glasgow regarded *The Wheel of Life* as a failure,[8] she
repeated its theme—love as transcendent of selfish passion—in her
next several books. In 1908 *The Ancient Law* explored the possibility of
a man's living a fulfilled life beyond any ordinary physical passion. It
chronicles what might have been an absorbing love between Daniel
Ordway Smith and Emily Brooks, a love which culminates instead with
all personal love relinquished to the larger love for all humankind.

Glasgow introduces Smith returning from prison as a wronged man
now motivated by a hard-won "vision of service."[9] Beginning life anew,
he assumes a different name and identity and acts as bookkeeper, legal
counsel, and minister to the simple people of Tappahannock; for a time
he succeeds in living "the life which would find its centre not in possession, but in surrender, which would seek as its achievement not personal happiness but the joy of service" (61). Smith's life fails to move
the reader, however, because of the number of melodramatic events
Glasgow marshals.

That Glasgow chose not to reprint either of these books in any later
edition is probably evidence enough that they were among her least successful novels. Their theme, however, was of great personal importance
and, one might suppose, comfort; writing these novels may have helped
her to bear the "mountain of grief" which was accumulating during
these important years. The quality of the writing she published between 1906 and 1909 reminds one of her explanation in *The Woman
Within* of the relationship between her own physical and mental state
and her ability to write really well:

> In periods of profound sorrow or of intense intellectual activity
> that is unallied to imagination, my power to create characters or to
> invest a theme with concrete images has deserted me. And when
> ever this power is lost, it can be recaptured only through meditation
> and reveries that are unforced and unrestrained.[10]

As Godbold points out, these are the years of Glasgow's interest in East-
ern and mystical thought: she was reading the *Bhagavad-Gita* and
Thomas à Kempis' *Imitation of Christ*, along with Nietzsche and Scho-
penhauer.[11] In letters, she repeatedly quotes from the Upanishads and
Buddhist proverbs, and states in a 1905 letter: "The truth remains that

in the roughest place in my life, I was brought back to some kind of acceptance and reconciliation wholly through an interest in the most abstruse and transcendental metaphysics in existence which is that of the sacred books of the East" (*L.*, 50).

The characters of Glasgow's next novels, the 1909 *The Romance of a Plain Man* and, in 1911, *The Miller of Old Church*, may have been reflections of her necessity to escape reality; each novel, however, despite its title, includes strong female characters and somewhat atypical social situations. Glasgow appears to be investigating even here the conventions and attitudes of most interest to women at the turn of the century.

The Romance of a Plain Man opens with an abused wife, Sarah Mickleborough, running from her drunken husband. Her child, Sally, offends the young Ben Starr, to whose cottage they have come for shelter during a storm, by calling him "common." Paralleling *The Voice of the People*, this novel follows the lives of Sally and Ben as Ben educates himself and claims his childhood love, fulfilling what he had referred to as his moving "straight toward a single love." [12] Unfortunately for the couple's happiness, Starr had also directed himself toward a "single ambition," and in pursuit of financial success, he pushes Sally toward the old friend who has consistently loved her. When Starr is finally faced with a necessary choice, to save Sally for himself or lose her to her friend, he gives up all business ambition and lives only for his love for his wife.

Conventional as the plot line may be, *The Romance of a Plain Man* is filled with interesting characters and situations. Sally's mother, fleeing her husband, lingers in the reader's mind as "a small frightened animal" (12), and the recurring imagery of stray dogs and cats, and Ben's helping a dying horse pull a cart uphill, shows Glasgow's strong sense of affinity between deprived and burdened animals and human beings. (It is Ben's act with the horse that wins Sally.) Once reared by her maiden aunts, Mitty and Matoaca Bland, Sally faces the contrast between the righteous convention of the Southern woman, in the person of Aunt Mitty, and what appears to be the feminist viewpoint, that of Miss Matoaca. In her 1938 preface to this novel, Glasgow defines "suffragist" as "having a vote, but never, never, no matter how tired you might be, having a man offer you either his arm or a chair" (viii). For Matoaca to refuse her fiancé because of his lack of honor toward a woman he had known previously cast her as spinster the rest of her life; early in the novel, Glasgow appears to find this stance admirable. Matoaca's attitudes are set against those of Mitty and the cheerful Mrs. Chitling with evident authorial approval: as Mrs. Chitling said so decisively,

I like a man that knows a woman's place, an' I like a woman that knows it, too. . . . What can she have, I ax, any mo' than she's got? Ain't she got everything already that the men don't want? Ain't sweetness an' virtue, an' patience an' long-suffering an' childbearin' enough for her without her impudently standin' up in the face of men an' axin' for mo'? Had she rather have a vote than the respect of men, an' ain't the respect of men enough to fill any honest woman's life? (64)

Yet when both Mitty and Matoaca refuse to receive Ben Starr, and later to allow Sally to marry him, Matoaca's liberality is seen as a sham, an attitude as provincial as those antifeminist sentiments voiced by the General: "But what would you do with a vote, my dear Miss Matoaca? Put it into a pie?" (77).

Glasgow speaks positively for the feminist position by creating the character of Sally Starr, whose life is directed by her own thinking about her choices, and who refuses to be bound by conventional concerns of position or finance. The ending of *The Romance of a Plain Man* is her exoneration.

The Miller of Old Church follows somewhat the same set of themes. Here, two people rise socially: Molly Merryweather, illegitimate daughter of Jonathan Gay, and the miller of the title, Abel Revercomb. Glasgow's sympathies are clear when she announces early in the book, in the words of the ineffectual but landed Jonathan Gay,

The miller Revercomb is a good example, I imagine, of just the thing you are speaking of, a kind of new plant which has sprung up like fire-weed out of the ashes. A quarter of a century produced him, but he's here to stay, of that I am positive. . . . He, or the stock he represents, of course, is already getting hold of the soil, and his descendants will run the state financially as well as politically, I suppose. We can't hold on, the rest of us—we're losing grip. [13]

Although the theme of effete gentility versus natively rooted energy again dominates this novel, more of Glasgow's attention in *The Miller of Old Church* falls on the conflict between traditional roles for women and the reality of a woman's emotional life. This 1911 novel, dedicated as it is to Cary with thanks for her support, is important for Glasgow's development because it gives her a way to combine the study of class change with the study of woman's role in the custom-bound South. Female characters in the novel include the maiden lady too late freed from family obligations (Kesiah, Jonathan Gay's aunt, would-be artist); the protected genteel mother, whose ignorance of life enervates and eventually destroys her family (Mrs. Gay); the young women whose lives exist only for fulfillment in romance (Judy Hatch Revercomb, Blossom Revercomb); and the heroine Molly Merryweather, whose difference from the conventional young girl is established early when she says impatiently,

> No, no, it isn't a man. Why do you seem to think that the beginning and middle and end of my existence is a man? There are times when I find even a turkey more interesting. (133)

In case the reader fails to understand just how radical Molly's attitudes are, Glasgow has provided a full text of "the womanly woman" in one of the Reverend Mullen's "most impressive sermons":

> Woman . . . was created to look after the ways of her household in order that man might go out into the world and make a career. No womanly woman cared to make a career. What the womanly woman desired was to remain an Incentive, an Ideal, an Inspiration. If the womanly woman possessed a talent, she did not use it, for this would unsex her; she sacrificed it in herself in order that she might return it to the race through her sons. Self-sacrifice, to use a worn metaphor, self-sacrifice was the breath of the nostrils of the womanly woman. It was for her power of self-sacrifice that men loved her and made an Ideal of her. Whatever else woman gave up, she must always retain her power of self-sacrifice if she expected the heart of her husband to rejoice in her. The home was founded on sacrifice, and woman was the pillar and the ornament of the home. There was her sphere, her purpose, her mission. All things outside that sphere belonged to man, except the privilege of ministering to the sick and the afflicted in other households. (100)

Glasgow's narrative skill here lies in playing off the traditions of romance—in which the denouement of the love relationships provides the central plot—with an interrogation of that tradition itself. In this novel many relationships illustrate her questioning of tradition. Her ironic deflation of the Ideal begins with the Reverend Mullen himself, who is much more interested in the beautiful women of his parish than he is in the self-sacrificing Judy Hatch, and continues throughout most of the relationships in the novel. Her focus on the debasing quality of most situations men have found pleasing—under the guise of their love for mother, tradition, family—makes clear her view that women have to begin thinking for themselves. Just as a recurring line in *The Romance of a Plain Man* was Sally's great-grandmother asking her husband how she felt, so the dependent woman comes in for a share of Glasgow's irony.

The innovation in this novel, so far as relationships are concerned, is the emphasis on friendships among women. One of the strongest scenes of the novel is that between Molly and Blossom, on Molly's discovery of Jonathan and Blossom's secret marriage. The dialogue is stark:

"Tell me, Blossom. Tell Molly," said the soft voice again.
"Molly!" he said sharply, and as she looked at him over
Blossom's prostrate head, he met a light of anger that seemed,
while it lasted, to illumine her features.
"Blossom and I were married nearly two years ago," he said.
"Nearly two years ago?" she repeated. "Why have we never
known it?"
"I had to think of my mother," he replied almost doggedly.

Glasgow uses this scene to make a didactic extension, as if the point were too important to leave to the reader's own comprehension. As Molly comforts Blossom, the explication insists:

The relation of woman to man was dwarfed suddenly by an understanding of the relation of woman to woman. Deeper than the dependence of sex, simpler, more natural, closer to the earth, as if it
still drew its strength from the soil, he realized that the need of
woman for woman was not written in the songs and the histories of
men, but in the neglected and frustrated lives which the songs and
the histories of men had ignored. (321)

Much of Glasgow's later fiction was an effort to present and illumi-nate those neglected and frustrated lives, and in that respect *Virginia* is one of her most important novels.

The title of Glasgow's tenth novel was meant to be suggestive of sev-eral ideas. By 1913, the year of *Virginia*'s publication, Glasgow had de-veloped some concept of her fiction as a chronology, or history, of her native state. She had spoken of this briefly but gives a more complete statement in the 1938 prefaces for the Virginia Edition.[14] More impor-tantly, the title implies an ideal female, a woman named reverentially after the land, serving the expected female functions of earth-mother, child-bearer, mythic and actual home. (In *The Battle-Ground* Glasgow had named Betty Ambler's beloved, passive sister "Virginia." She later dedicates the novel *Virginia* to her "radiant spirit" of a sister, Cary Mc-Cormack, who had died in 1911 after being widowed in her twenties.) The tragic ending of the novel *Virginia* shows Glasgow's view of the pathos of this proud Southern woman, "cut out for happiness" yet fated to exist so unhappily. And of course the name Virginia itself suggests the index of purity, the condition of virginity by which so many women have been judged, both in life and literature.

With Glasgow's personal interest in the options open to women, she appears to have found new impetus to write once she turned more frequently to using women characters as protagonists. With the character of Virginia she could once again emphasize the inherent trap in a woman's conforming to social expectations—the dangers of being dutiful, obeisant, and subordinate. Glasgow described Virginia as a character embodying "the Victorian ideal for whom love was enough." [15]

As Glasgow explained in the preface, she had meant to depict Virginia ironically, since she herself had not followed the conventions of proper Virginia life. Once into the novel, however, "my irony grew fainter while it yielded at last to sympathetic compassion. By the time I had approached the end, the simple goodness of Virginia's manners had turned a comedy of manners into a tragedy of human fate" (x). Because Glasgow was creating a character who was painfully familiar to her (in the personae of her mother, her sister Cary, and many other Richmond women), her identification with Virginia was complete: "I knew her life as well as if I had lived it in her place, hour by hour, day by day, week by week" (x). "Virginia . . . was the evocation of an ideal and is always associated with my mother and the women of her period. I describe Virginia in the beginning exactly as I was told my mother looked when she was a girl" (*L.*, 131).

Some of Glasgow's best prose up to this time appears in *Virginia*, and her heightened fictional power results at least in part from her intense personal identification with the female characters. Another writer might have been content to view this study as a "novel of manners": women's lives are excellent for showing religion, family, customs, the foibles of the times. But in this case, and increasingly in Glasgow's fiction, that insulating perspective—that what one writes, particularly about women, serves primarily a sociological function—gave way to a more truthful admission: Glasgow was writing about the lives of Virginia

women because those lives had shaped hers. As a maverick—albeit
a demure one—Glasgow saw the real repression inherent in the code
of behavior.

> I could not separate Virginia from her background, because she was
> an integral part of it, and it shared her vitality. What she was, that
> background and atmosphere had helped to make her. . . . Every
> person in Dinwiddie, from the greatest to the least, was linked . . .
> with her tragedy and with the larger tyranny of tradition. (xii)

And so the novel—which opens with Virginia as beguiling young
woman, intent only on loving well—becomes a chronological portrayal
of the self-effacing stages in a good woman's life. It shows as well the
final *reductio ad absurdum* of that self-effacement. Virginia has listened
carefully to the sermons of the Reverend Mullen. She has heeded the
admonitions of her mother and her only teacher, the spinster Miss Pris-
cilla Batte, who was "capable of dying for an idea, but not of conceiving
one" (10). The first third of the novel, captioned "The Dream," summarizes Virginia's education as she becomes a good wife and mother.
Even though Glasgow has described the loss of personality of Lucy Pendleton, Virginia's weary mother, Virginia is never warned. She ignores
the example of her mother's life and speaks with "a glorious certainty"
about her own future as Oliver's wife.

Glasgow shows within the novel, however, that the Pendleton blind-
ness is more than a feminine trait. All the Pendletons see life as they
want it to be rather than as it is:

> The three stood in silence, gazing dreamily, with three pairs of Pen-
> dleton eyes, down toward the site of the old slave market. Directly
> in their line of vision, an overladen mule with a sore shoulder was
> straining painfully under the lash, but none of them saw it, because
> each of them was morally incapable of looking an unpleasant fact in
> the face, if there was any honourable manner of avoiding it. (51)

Given Glasgow's sensitivity to the treatment of animals, their faulty vision in this scene is particularly damning.

That this idealism carried over to romantic love was to be expected.
It is but a few pages further on that Virginia sees Oliver Treadwell and
experiences "delicious embarrassment" as "little thrills of joy, like tiny
flames, ran over her." This is the girl who can ask her mother, "Love is

the only thing that really matters, isn't it, mother?" and be answered, "A pure and noble love, darling. It is a woman's life. God meant it so" (154). Sanctioned by church as well as a range of cultural attitudes, women's submission was a given. There is little hope that the liberal, educated Oliver Treadwell—so fascinated by the perfection of Virginia's unsophisticated love—can remain long enamored of her limited personality. One of the ironies of the novel is that Treadwell himself knows her limitations, as when he teases her in the early marketing scene:

> "I've always had a tremendous sympathy for women because they have to market and housekeep. I wonder if they won't revolt some time?"
> This was so heretical a point of view that she tried earnestly to comprehend it; but all the time her heart was busy telling her how different he was from every other man, how much more interesting! how immeasurably superior! . . . Seeing that he was waiting for a response, she made a violent endeavour to think of one, and uttered almost inaudibly: "But don't they like it?"
> "Ah, that's just it," he answered as seriously as if she hadn't known that her speech bordered on imbecility. "Do they really like it? or have they been throwing dust in our eyes through the centuries?" And he gazed at her as eagerly as if he were hanging upon her answer. Oh, if she could only say something clever! If she could only say the sort of thing that would shock Miss Priscilla! But nothing came of her wish, and she was reduced at last to the pathetic rejoinder, "I don't know. I'm afraid I've never thought about it." (56)

Relegating Virginia to the same unthinking posture as the women before her serves to alert the reader to the dangers of her tenuous position as Oliver's wife. Glasgow uses comparison throughout the novel with Susan Treadwell, Oliver's cousin and Virginia's girlhood friend, to make the contrast all the clearer.

Part two of *Virginia* chronicles "The Reality." Once married and living apart from her parents, Virginia writes them intimate details of her life with Oliver, and of the birth of their first child. Glasgow's epistolary method vividly conveys the voice of the naïve, unthinking woman: "I try not to let Oliver see how I mind it. He has so much to bother him, poor dear, that I keep all of my worries, big and little, in the background. When anything goes wrong in the house I never tell him" (164).

Oliver and I are never apart for a single minute except when he is at work in the office. He hasn't written a line since we came here, but he's going to begin as soon as we get settled, and then he says that I may sit in the room and sew if I want to. I can't believe that people really love each other unless they want to be together every instant no matter what they are doing. (167)

I haven't let the baby out of my sight because I wouldn't trust Daisy with her for anything in the world. She is so terribly flighty. I have the crib brought into my room (though Oliver hates it) and I take entire charge of her night and day. I should love to do it if only Oliver didn't mind it so much. . . . he doesn't know (for I never tell him) how very tired I am by the time night comes. Sometimes when Oliver comes home and we sit in the dining-room (we never use the drawing-room because it is across the hall and I'm afraid I shouldn't hear the baby cry) it is as much as I can do to keep my eyes open. I try not to let him notice it, but one night when he read me the first act of a play he is writing, I went to sleep, and though he didn't say anything, I could see that he was very much hurt. (173, 175)

Playwright and man of letters that Oliver is, Virginia's total disinterest in his work stifles their relationship even more quickly than had her self-imposed duties as mother. To Virginia and other women trained to revere the physical comforts they should provide, art is inconsequential. As she thought when Oliver was emotionally broken by the bad reviews of his first New York play,

If only he would stop trying to pretend that he was not miserable and that nothing had happened! After all, it couldn't be so very bad, could it? It wasn't in the least as if one of the children were ill. (221)

Glasgow manages to save what might have been a mawkish situation by giving Virginia the insight, eventually, to realize what has happened: she has been trained to be a superb wife through self-sacrifice and devotion to her children and parents. That this ethos was of little relevance to a liberally educated man like Oliver did not strike her until half a dozen years after their marriage, when she forces herself to admit, "Love, which had seemed to her to solve all problems and smooth all difficulties, was helpless to enlighten her. It was not love; it was something else that she needed now, and of this something else she knew not even so much as the name" (221).

The remainder of part two shows Virginia collecting her talents, readying her will for the contest, and keeping Oliver from Abby Good, the educated predator who is conversant with both the theater and Oliver's dreams about it. Glasgow in her preface speaks accurately about the force of Virginia as character, as being a woman more misled than incompetent:

> The pathos of it was that neither in life nor in my novel was she a weak character, as some undiscerning readers have called her. On the contrary, she was a woman whose vital energy had been deflected, by precept and example, into a single emotional centre. She was, indeed, as I had known her prototype in one I loved and pitied, the logical result of an inordinate sense of duty, the crowning achievement of the code of beautiful behaviour and the Episcopal Church. (xii–xiii)

The rest of the novel is a series of drawn battles—a few magnificent scenes in which Virginia borrows a horse and joins Abby and Oliver riding, emerging the victor—but each personal victory is undercut by the force of family circumstances. She must give up a trip with the would-be lovers because her son is dying of diphtheria: life for Virginia poses no choices, only command performances. Her conception of what being a wife and mother means absorbs all her strength and potential as a human being.

Glasgow opens the third and last section, "The Adjustment," just after the death of Gabriel, Virginia's father. Bereft of paternal support, Virginia stops questioning the roles she must—of training and inclination—play; consequently, she eventually loses Oliver to a young New York actress, Margaret Oldcastle. Virginia's behavior throughout the estrangement is, once again, self-effacing and admirable, but Glasgow darkens our view of Virginia's nobility at this point in her life by presenting it as cowardice. Virginia could confront neither Margaret with her sins nor Oliver with his weaknesses; neither could she take her own life.

> She felt suddenly that even the passive courage which was hers, the courage of endurance, had deserted her. She saw the dreadful hours that must ensue before she went back to Dinwiddie, the dreadful days that would follow after she got there, the dreadful weeks that

would run on into the dreadful years. Silent, gray, and endless, they stretched ahead of her, and through them all she saw herself, a little hopeless figure, moving toward the death which she had not had the courage to die. (403)

That any woman, regardless of her place in history, assumes death as a viable alternative to the loss of a husband is further proof of the cultural debilitation women's education promotes. Glasgow had worked with this situation in her 1902 novel, *The Battle-Ground*, showing Betty Ambler's mother waste into death after her husband was killed during the Civil War: "Mrs. Ambler . . . seemed at last to be gently withdrawing from a place in which she found herself a stranger. There was nothing to detain her now; she was too heartsick to adapt herself to many changes; loss and approaching poverty might be borne by one for whom the chief thing yet remained; but she had seen this go, and so she waited, with her pensive smile, for the moment when she too might follow." [16]

Neither Mrs. Ambler's nor Virginia's finale resembles the "happy ending" that their expectations might have suggested. In deference to the fact that Virginia Pendleton Treadwell had lived so honorably— given the confines of familial and social opinion in which she lived— Glasgow allows her the loyalty of her children: once she returns from New York and recognizes that she cannot fight for Oliver, a telegram from her son arrives: "Dearest mother, I am coming home to you" (406). Whether or not child for husband is a fair exchange is not the consideration; Virginia did, at least for a time, escape the bottomless loneliness of which she was so afraid.

The tragedy of Virginia is very much as Glasgow describes it in the preface, the tragedy of "a single dream of identity" (xxi). Speaking from the vantage point of 1938, when the preface was written, Glasgow was well aware of the importance of *Virginia* to her later writing, and to her personal life. No subsequent Glasgow heroine was ever so monochromatic.

Early notes for the novel show that the original *Virginia* was to have two heroines. Virginia Pendleton was to be contrasted throughout with Sarah Jane Treadwell, whose clear-headed independence made her an atypical Southern girl. Introduced as a pair early in the novel, Virginia and Sarah Jane (Susan Treadwell in the published version) lead outwardly parallel lives: both marry, have children, and remain in Dinwiddie. Sarah Jane's marriage, however, never dominates her life. She succeeds in being herself at least partly because, as Glasgow notes, she is "the woman who sees men and things as they are and accepts them with humorous sympathy." In contrast, Virginia "idealises them and is impatient of imperfection." One chapter title is given as "The Wisdom of Sarah Jane," who is referred to in the text as "the softened intellectual." She is "the actual"; Virginia is "the ideal."[17] In a later series of notes, Sarah Jane has been renamed Sue, and Glasgow explains as further contrast that Virginia was exhausted ("life had worn her out and left her only a shell") whereas "Sue, with her six children had kept her youth and her interests; but then, Sue had never given herself—The inviobility [sic] of her soul had preserved the freshness of her body."[18]

Besides Sarah Jane/Susan, other interesting women are suggested in Glasgow's notes. Mrs. Tom Peachy is evidently intended to be a strong character rather than a comic one; Mrs. Treadwell, a much misused one; and Margaret Auld, a highly sympathetic woman who tries to deny her love for Oliver (the reader may sense an autobiographical note as Glasgow tries to justify the love between the beautiful but lonely actress and the married Oliver).[19] Glasgow was clearly bent on picturing some women as self-achieving; that tone of affirmation also permeates the character of Virginia who, at one point, is seen as the martyr only to her demanding children.

Most interesting of all, Glasgow attempts in one series of notes to create a triumphant ending for the deserted Virginia. Similar in tone to the conclusion of *Barren Ground* a decade later, this ending stresses Virginia's recognition of her bereavement but, instead of sorrow, her loss leads to new hope and strength:

> Hope sang again like an imprisoned bird in her breast—She felt herself strong to face life—To pity, to suffer & to love in the future as she had pitied, suffered & loved in the past—. . . .
> The magic & the exaltation of first love pulsed was returned to her in her veins while she stood there. . . . She smelt the scent of honey suckle blooming on that June afternoon . . . thirty years ago.[20]

Clearly inappropriate to Virginia's state of mind after she loses Oliver, · this ending instead suggests Glasgow's own need to derive joy and serenity from her own isolation. Her renunciation of lovers and fiancés must have been tempered constantly with those fears of loneliness which she attributes to Virginia; the strength of her characterization stemmed at least partly from Glasgow's own self-understanding.

Extensive sections of *Virginia* were also slated to tell the story of Cyrus Treadwell, Sarah Jane's father, a wealthy but brutally unfeeling Southern businessman. As Oliver Steele points out,

> It is clear that at first she planned for him to have an importance in the structure of the novel which would have meant significant changes in his character and, indeed, in the theme of the book. . . . She planned a history of Cyrus' rise to power which was to run parallel to Virginia's story. . . . Almost none of this finds place in the final version of *Virginia*. . . . She must have seen that so elaborate a treatment of Cyrus and the public victory of commerce and materialism over aristocratic idealism could only weaken the effect of what was from the first her main interest, the character and fate of Virginia.[21]

That Glasgow relinquished this story line—and with it her announced theme of "transition from an aristocratic to a commercial civilization"[22]—was a major shift in narrative strategy. With this turn, in *Virginia*, to an admitted focus on woman as protagonist and on the theme of woman's fulfillment in, at best, a restrictive culture, Glasgow began in earnest the study which had appeared intermittently throughout her earlier fiction. That this focus was conscious becomes clear in her 1916 interview with Overton:

> When I began *Virginia* I had in mind three books dealing with the adjustment of human lives to changing conditions.
>   In *Virginia* I wanted to do the biography of a woman, representative of the old system of chivalry and showing her relation to that system and the changing order. Virginia's education . . . was designed to paralyze her reasoning faculties and to eliminate all danger of mental unsettling. Virginia was the passive and helpless victim of the ideal of feminine self-sacrifice. The circumstances of her life first molded and then dominated her.[23]

There is little question that this period of Glasgow's fiction—from the end of her affair with Gerald B. in either 1905 or 1906 to the publication of *Virginia* in 1913—is both interesting in itself and crucial for determining the direction of her later fully mature work.

CHAPTER 4

The Years of the Locust

Whether or not Glasgow was conscious at the time of its publication of the power of *Virginia*, or of its implications about her theories of fiction, later critics clearly recognized the importance of the novel. Anne Firor Scott sees it as a wonderfully accurate exposé of the image of the genteel woman ("Few more biting criticisms of the image are in print") and, perhaps more important, of the culture that conditioned such a woman.

> Virginia, the youthful heroine of the book, was just of marriageable age at its beginning, and she held firmly to the romantic illusion that for *her* the world must hold wonders yet unseen. Miss Glasgow, of course, knew better, and showed it, in the sharply etched pictures of marriage in Dinwiddie. She touched on all the sorest points: the mulatto child of the leading citizen, the inability of many southern men to appreciate a strong woman, the drunkard whose courageous wife kept a boarding-house and never spoke of his inability to make a living.[1]

For J. R. Raper, *Virginia* paralleled Melville's great novella: "*Virginia*, an anatomy of the virgin mind, was perhaps the best informed and least mitigated fictional assault on American innocence since Melville's *Benito Cereno*. Within the limits of one character's life and town, it manages to suggest something of the sexual, familial, artistic, racial, and economic tragedies of a nation of people who innocently assume that idealism is a moral position and forget that, at base, it is an ontological commitment which they lack the courage or (in Dinwiddie, at least) the intelligence to examine."[2]

For all her reading in philosophy, Glasgow seems to have been motivated much more directly in this novel by her convictions about the immediate human condition, and these convictions led in one way to new concepts for her about the role of the novel. As she was to explain a few years later,

> Even in the novel, we are beginning to demand a larger presentment of life than may be condensed into a formalized depiction of

love. We are beginning, indeed, to demand a faithful rendering of existence, and a more pointed analysis of our emotions, as well as a closer and more sceptical examination of accepted facts. . . . With all its faults and failings, the contemporary novel remains alive, however inadequately; and, from my point of view, even inadequacy is redeemed by the eagerness with which this vital medium strives for a more intense consciousness, and for a closer agreement with the realities of experience.[3]

Glasgow's statement implies that her fiction may have been a means of analyzing her emotions. Particularly in times of personal anguish, she may have been motivated by the necessity of working through feelings, including anger, which she may not have admitted consciously to herself. Both Scott and Raper, for example, point out that in *Virginia* the character of Cyrus Treadwell resembles Glasgow's autocratic father, and that if the character of Mrs. Treadwell is meant to represent that of Glasgow's mother, it is sad testimony indeed to the parental relationship.[4] The identification between the character Susan Treadwell and Glasgow herself has already been suggested, as has that between Virginia and Glasgow's sister Cary (who was a younger version of her beloved mother). To a greater extent than ever before, it seems likely that in *Virginia* Glasgow was using her fiction to plumb areas too painful to investigate consciously.

It is also possible that characterization in *Virginia* was a means of wish-fulfillment on Glasgow's part. Her personal choices in life show that—no matter what her rhetoric—she found being fully independent difficult. Much as she appears to have admired characters like Betty Ambler and Susan Treadwell in her fiction, one senses a contradiction. As Barbro Ekman points out,

Glasgow had rebelled against the convictions of her day. The women she admires are strong and able to live without love; yet, deep at heart, they all, including Glasgow, seem to think that love is the only thing worth having.[5]

Part of the vacillation that marks her female characters is probably Glasgow's own indecision: much of her personal response to life was, and should have been, that of the traditional Southern gentlewoman she so often censured. As Godbold states, "Ellen herself was one day an old-fashioned Southern girl and the next day a modern intellectual. . . . In all of her life she was not able to shed either role, nor was she able to reconcile them."[6]

In Glasgow's interview with Overton, she describes *Virginia* as the first of a series of three novels dealing with women protagonists. Virginia, with her paralyzing education, was at one end of a continuum Glasgow was creating as she both wrote and lived. Who knew how far the other end would reach? The second stage of modern female education was to have been illustrated by Gabriella Carr in *Life and Gabriella*. As Glasgow described that character:

> Gabriella was the product of the same school, but instead of being used by circumstances, she used them to create her own destiny. . . . Gabriella had the courage of action and through molding circumstances wrested from life her happiness and success.[7]

Traits given to Susan Treadwell in *Virginia* are here those which make possible Gabriella's accomplishment—the development of independence with direction—but Glasgow, as late as 1916, seemed to realize that this kind of character was not fully emancipated. Gabriella too was prone to romantic fantasies, but she also knew that life could not be lived entirely on emotional response:

> The mistake women, wives, have always made is that they have concentrated too intensely on emotion. Husband and wife must be mentally companionable if their happiness is to last through the years.[8]

Glasgow uses happiness as an index of Virginia Pendleton's motivation as well, but she sees Virginia as undermining her own possible strength through her willingness to sacrifice: "Virginia desired happiness but did not expect it, much less fight for it, and consequently in a system where self-sacrifice was the ideal of womanhood she became submerged by circumstances."[9]

Life and Gabriella is, then, well titled, for the battle as Glasgow saw it waged is between woman and "circumstances," the sum total of cultural attitudes, social expectations, religious formulae—these forces almost independent of sexual or personal motivation. In this novel the strong woman protagonist, self-sufficient, unafraid of either work or social attitudes, differs from the heroines of Glasgow's earlier fiction. Part of the difference stems from the fact that Gabriella lives in New York, far from the conventions which would prohibit her working and rearing her children alone. Isolated as she is from friends and family, she can also maintain a friendship with Ben O'Hara, even if his social position is inferior to hers.

Glasgow's eleventh novel is the product of her personal voyage to independence. Having left Richmond after Cary's death, Glasgow lived in New York. Distraught by the family deaths, however, she found that leaving her home was more difficult than she would have expected; in fact, once she had begun writing the novel which was to be *Virginia*, she had to return to that state in order to write well. Both the theme of the 1913 novel and her need to write in familiar surroundings appear to have surprised Glasgow; she recalls in *The Woman Within*,

> The idea for *Virginia* pushed its way to the surface of thought; but I soon discovered that the characters would not come to life in New York. They needed their own place and soil and atmosphere; and after a brief and futile resistance, I went back, for a visit to old Petersburg, which is the Dinwiddie of my novel. . . . I could not write in New York. (195)

For all her emphasis on rationality, Glasgow was consistently motivated by nonintellectual decisions. Once again, her impulsive nature dominated her life—she had left home, and then returned home to write the Virginia novels. Finally, she returned to Richmond for good. Some insight into her personality comes from her 1905 comment to Mary Johnston:

> You are so different from me in many ways, and particularly in as much as you keep your impulses so firmly in hand while mine so often carry me breathlessly away. (*L.*, 46)

Whether or not Glasgow's Arien sun sign gave her this bent toward relatively rash action (as well as her interest in astrology and the occult), Glasgow's pattern was to decide quickly, instinctively, on courses of action. Even in her relationships with people, she formed early judgments. She had immediately liked Mary Johnston, Marjorie Kinnan Rawlings, Signe Toksvig; her subsequent letters to them show that she quickly became intimate with people she liked.[10] Her relationships with men seemed similar: she writes in *The Woman Within* of her "love-at-first-sight" situation with Gerald B., and the courtship with Henry Anderson was also spontaneous. Her definition of "love" as "madness" also supports these personality traits of impulsiveness and openness:

> I have felt grateful to anyone who has sincerely cared for me. But gratitude, though noble in sentiment, is without madness; and madness is the very essence of falling in love. (179)

Responsive by this time of her life to instinctive choices in her writing as well, Glasgow could be content to have novels appear—or, rather, the characters in them—as she described the process of her being found by the characters of her fiction. Once Glasgow felt that she had been "given" a character—for instance, that of Virginia—she allowed the tone of her work to reflect the mood that character evoked. She speaks of *Virginia* as being the first of her mature novels, the beginning of her process of taking the "complete plunge."[11] Not only had she realized that "all creative writing is an extension of personality," she had learned as well that the variable of personality had to be allowed. "Life to me has been a continuous becoming," she writes.[12] The satisfaction which Glasgow feels as she is writing the Virginia Edition prefaces in 1938 stems partly from her sense of control over both her craft and her life: "I feel younger at 60 than I did at 20," she writes in the preface to *Life and Gabriella* (xv).

In retrospect, Glasgow explained that as long as she had been completely absorbed in her own life, she was in a sense distracted from her writing. "Something, either joy or pain, had come between me and my single-minded devotion to craftsmanship. . . . Without admitting it, I had felt, at times, that I was writing not with the whole of myself, but with some second personality. When I was in love with Gerald, I used to think: 'Some day, when I am older, and living is less intense, I shall be able to put the whole of myself into my work. Then I shall ripen into the artist I have it in me to be'" (*WW*, 181).

It seems obvious that *Virginia* was Glasgow's response to the tutelage of her family and culture, evoked bitterly once she had witnessed Cary's self-sacrificing existence to her early death. In many ways *Life and Gabriella* is another response to the same sets of expectations spawned by the Southern family/church/culture. Glasgow's emphasis in her title, however, changes direction: life, not death, is to be Gabriella's prize; and the novel was subtitled, "The Story of a Woman's Courage."[13]

The process of Gabriella's coming to independence dominates the first half of the novel. *Life and Gabriella* opens in "The Age of Faith," a period in which Gabriella questions and breaks one engagement, but then falls in love with and marries George Fowler. Even though she has begun what appears to be a conventional pattern for a romance, Glasgow has used her opening chapters to emphasize the differences among Gabriella and her mother (the greatest romantic of them all, who wears mourning sixteen years after her husband's death), her sister Jane (fleeing from, yet eager to reconcile with, her abusive husband), and the majority of her family's womenfolk. Yet once Gabriella has become engaged to George, her behavior changes radically; she too comes to believe, "There is nothing but love in the world" (97). Too soon after marriage, however, she realizes that

> as far as character and experience counted, she was immeasurably older than George. Her superior common sense made her feel almost middle-aged when he was in one of his boyish moods. At the age of nine she had not been so utterly irresponsible as George was at twenty-six; as an infant in arms she probably regarded the universe with a profounder philosophy. . . . Gabriella loved him, she had chosen him, she told herself now, and she meant to abide by her choice; but she was not blind, she was not a fool, and she was deficient in the kind of loyalty which obliges one to lie even in the sanctity of one's own mind. She would be true to him, but she would be true with her eyes open, not shut. (129)

Once Gabriella's daughter is born, she is caught in a maze of dependency, financial as well as emotional, only to realize that George likes drink and other women too well. Glasgow laments, "She was barely twenty-two and love was over for ever" (166). This realization ends "The Age of Faith" and slants the novel dangerously near the domestic category.[14]

"The Age of Knowledge," the second half of the novel, is devoted to developing the younger Gabriella, the woman of "native energy and independence" (vii). The title refers to her first "knowledge," that George has been unfaithful—has, in fact, left her for another woman. Gabriella's second "knowledge" comes through people's reactions to that event; the real personal strengths of various family members surprise her. The third and most important knowledge is of her own resources, as she finds work and rears her children on her own. Never bitter, Gabriella brings pleasure to these lives, even though her own existence is a round of work and effort, and a retreat to reminiscences of her early life. Glasgow had written in the preface to this novel that life was, ideally, to be a "continual becoming" (xv). Gabriella's failure, in this period, is that she has shut herself off from change; her primary action is maintaining, not becoming. She prefers her dream of an early lover to the companionship of the self-made Ben O'Hara, and even after realizing how wrong that choice has been, she still defers to Chance:

> As soon as I meet him—and in the end I shall surely meet him— everything will be right. (417)

Once she finds O'Hara gone, however, Gabriella does follow him, the thought of impropriety much less threatening than the danger of losing him. Glasgow uses this scene as the image of Gabriella's "strength, her firmness, her courage, and of her belief in life" (420). It is also, however, a scene of compromise: Gabriella has found a man she can admire and love; she will marry him and live happily ever after. Her independence and strength have brought her the reward of Ben O'Hara—a man, a mate—so that *Life and Gabriella* has ended as a highly conventional romance, with a highly conventional ending.

John Cawelti defines a romance as being much more than a novel about a woman. As he writes in *Adventure, Mystery, and Romance*,

> The crucial defining characteristic of romance is not that it stars a female but that its organizing action is the development of a love relationship. . . . romances often contain elements of adventure but the dangers function as a means of challenging, then, cementing the love relationship. . . . the moral fantasy of the romance is that of love triumphant and permanently overcoming all obstacles and difficulties.[15]

Glasgow's intention was far beyond a conventional romance, as her emphasis on the woman's life separate from her romantic entanglements seems to show. Perhaps she would have been interested in Cawelti's distinctions while she was writing her prefaces in 1938, but in 1916, genre distinctions were far from occupying Glasgow's attention. Once *Life and Gabriella* appeared in January, 1916, Glasgow turned her energies to the move back to One West Main in Richmond. Her brother Arthur had seen to its redecorating after the death of their father, but Glasgow returned home with trepidation. As she later recalled of that spring, "I was alone, now, in the house where so many of us had once lived together. . . . I felt only phantoms. . . . At the time I saw only my desperate need of something—of anything to save me from the inescapable past" (*WW*, 215, 221). Glasgow's real physical loneliness was intensified both by her encroaching deafness and by her feelings of having exhausted her interest in writing. It was a worrisome spring, a bleak spring.

On Easter Sunday of that season a friend invited Glasgow to a small luncheon in order that she might meet Henry Anderson. Glasgow, then forty-two, was tempted to scoff at Anderson's airs of anglophilia and his obsession with social climbing. What she found, however, was a charming, articulate, forceful and well-read man who quickly became her suitor. That she fell in love with him seems apparent. Given her own peculiarly isolated situation, her feeling for him is easily explained; what is most interesting about the romance, in retrospect, is her vehemence about its unsuitability. Not only does Glasgow refer to the years of her courtship as "the years of the locust"; but she also calls the eventual twenty-year period a "comedy of errors" and reflects that the experience "killed my spirit, but it taught me much of the vast geography of human nature. When it was over, if it were ever over, I could travel, by instinct alone, through that 'dark wood' of the soul" (*WW*, 214–15). The rancor of these comments is reflected as well in her 1923 confession to Hugh Walpole about this period:

> After I wrote *Life and Gabriella* about 8 or 10 years ago, I let go and gave up. I was passing through an experience that seemed to drain everything out of me—vitality, imagination, interest, everything. In that time I lost a great deal, and I slipped somehow, naturally I suppose, away from what I had won. Now, I have boiled up, I hope, out of those depths, and I am trying to win back what I have lost. (*L.*, 60)

Her reference in *The Woman Within* is to a twenty-year affair (if the affair had ever ended); here she refers to an eight- or ten-year hiatus. Scant as information is about the Anderson-Glasgow relationship, her own admission about the psychological effects of that situation can hardly be ignored.

Perhaps the most interesting point to be made about *Life and Gabriella* as one of Glasgow's mature novels, finally, is that it foreshadows Glasgow's own immediate circumstances. Like Gabriella, Glasgow too had been disappointed and ultimately unfulfilled in early romantic relationships. She too had accomplished a life for herself through work and talent: both Gabriella and Glasgow were successful. And both, at forty, felt that the urgency to continue pouring all their energies into their work had passed. The fictional Gabriella found Ben O'Hara and—after trying to love a well-born man whose effete life and sterility now only offended her—went away with him. Glasgow found Henry Anderson (and perhaps, before him, the Mulhern of her New York apartment).[16] These men were neighbors but never social equals. As the correspondence between Glasgow and Anderson suggests, there were moments when Glasgow too would have gone off with Anderson. While it seems clear that Glasgow was responsible for deciding (repeatedly, in fact) not to marry, what remains of Anderson's correspondence to her—Glasgow's letters to him were all destroyed—suggests that there were intervals when she longed for a situation more permanent than an engagement. The changes in the Anderson correspondence reflect the tensions operative in their relationship. An early (Sept. 13, 1916) letter from Anderson on board the R.M.S. *Adriatic* gives the tone of the preengagement letters:

> I think of you very constantly these days and what you say in your letter. If I have brightened your life, made its outlook more cheerful, you don't know how glad that makes me, for that above all things I long to do. . . . God forbid that I should ever do anything to mar or hurt it—I tremble before the possibility of such a thing.

By September 10 of 1920, however, the engagement had been made and broken several times (as Anderson writes in an undated letter, "The truth is, my dear, 'everything has been ended' so often that I sometimes am in doubt"), and Anderson's patience seems to be wearing thin.

> Nothing gives me more pleasure than to come to see you when we can be like two normal people—entirely natural—not living in strained situations or impossible discussions—Your former letter *did* make me very angry. I am sorry if I showed it. . . . These monthly climaxes have been a fearful drain on my nervous organization. . . . the truth is that my nerve strength is breaking under the strain of the last two years, and I am not equal to climaxes or discussions of that kind.

Again, in an undated letter, this reference to their "decision":

We determined then after many long and painful discussions to go on as we were, and I have tried to keep this agreement in letter and in spirit—I have no desire to change it now. . . .

I am sorry if I was dull last evening but I enjoyed the quiet of the porch and I think we both understand the blessing of just being quiet sometimes—I am willing to try to do anything, but if it be possible do not try to impose more burdens upon me now, for I am ill, and tired, and sometimes feel that life and its complications are already more than I can bear.

There are also many passages that read like the following, so that one senses that Anderson was continuously being accused of disappointing Glasgow; whether he did or not remains unknown. Glasgow's expectations may have been unreasonable; that point too remains unclear.

Since you have "turned away forever," I accept it, and go forth to face life as best I can, shadowed by one great failure. Yet I know in my conscience I have done my best—a poor best perhaps—but *my* best—my honest best![17]

The sheaves of Anderson's pale blue pages, imprinted with the "Nine Hundred and Thirteen West Franklin Street, Richmond, Virginia," attest to his consistency and his perseverance. The letters date from 1916 to 1945.

While the agony of the courtship and engagement at first dominated and then colored Glasgow's life for at least the next decade, she was conscious throughout of the cultural pressure to marry Anderson. Such was a woman's role. No matter what his motives or his earlier experiences, no matter that he had a flirtatious nature, Ellen Glasgow— particularly Ellen Glasgow in her mid-forties—should have been eager to accept him. Torn as she was between love for him and recognition of his less scrupulous qualities, she wrote not only *Barren Ground* (1925) but the trilogy of manners (*The Romantic Comedians*, 1926; *They Stooped to Folly*, 1929; and *The Sheltered Life*, 1932) under the impetus of her ambivalence about her courtship.[18] Once she had deigned to care about him, even to accept him (in July of 1917), his leaving her to court other women—first, Queen Marie; later, younger women—was an intolerable affront. Her poignant if perhaps too bitter account of the relationship is published in *The Woman Within*, except for the following italicized passage, which she deleted.

Several times in those years we parted forever, as we thought, but from some obscure cause the parting was never final. Always, the tie drew us together again. For twenty-one years, the bond held. *If I have told too much of those years, I can only insist that I have not told the one incredible fact which alone might explain the inconsistencies, and reduce the illogic.*[19]

Glasgow's feelings toward Anderson, at least early in their relationship, prompted the highly favorable characterizations of the male protagonists in *The Builders*, published in 1919, and in *One Man in His Time*, which appeared in 1922. David Blackburn, an "idealist, literally on fire with ideas,"[20] holds the reader's attention throughout *The Builders*. Glasgow opens the novel with Caroline Meade, a thirty-two-year-old nurse, whose life has spun to a stop after a broken engagement. "There must be something one can live on besides love," she thinks in an early scene (7). Once Caroline takes a position with the Blackburns and comes to love the much-maligned politician who is the dupe of his malevolent wife Angelica, Glasgow uses our interest in Caroline to further emphasize Blackburn's superiority. She identifies him with the "vein of iron" image used so importantly later, in both *Barren Ground* and *Vein of Iron* (there, to refer to female protagonists). Indeed, she mars the novel throughout by including long dialogues based on Blackburn-Anderson's political beliefs. The book's title comes from one of those passages in which Blackburn insists that men move from materialism to idealism, from wanting merely things to wanting better conditions:

I haven't a doubt that the frantic struggle in America to amass things, to make great fortunes, has led to discoveries of incalculable benefit to mankind. . . . This spirit, this single phase of development, is still serving a purpose. We have watched it open the earth, build railroads, establish industries, cut highways over mountains, turn deserts into populous cities; and through these things lay the foundation of the finer and larger social order—the greater national life. . . . It all comes back to the builders. We are . . . a nation of idealists. . . . Because we build in the sky, I believe we are building to last. (107–108)

Once abandoned by his wife and free to love Caroline, Blackburn instead goes to France to fight in World War I; when he eventually writes to Caroline—after a year abroad—it is a twenty-page political treatise.

(That Anderson was helping Glasgow write this novel is clear from the quantity and content of both these political passages and their feelings toward each other, already discussed.)[21] He praises her for being the kind of woman she is so that he is free to write of "the life of the mind," and he concludes with his promise to do "the best work of my life . . . just for my country" (357, 358). Even when he explains his decision to return to Angelica as being "unselfish patriotism" and "sacrifice for the general good," Caroline simply smiles and says "I understand" (376). Blackburn's reasoning and decision bring the novel to an incredible end, because Glasgow has done such an expert job in drawing Angelica as completely evil that Caroline is the only one Blackburn convinces. To be so poor a judge of people, Blackburn was an unusually lucky politician.

One Man in His Time, the next novel on which Anderson collaborated, reads as a sequel to. *The Builders*. Published in 1922, written in the years after the primary infatuation between Glasgow and Anderson, this novel has as leading male characters both the powerful new governor of Virginia, Gideon Vetch, and elitist John Benham, the politician defeated in that contest. Benham seems for a time to win Corinna Page, the clear heroine of the novel; Vetch dies a martyr for political freedom. Glasgow's sympathy moves between Vetch and Benham, one man born in a circus tent and the other an aristocrat whose highly civilized life has drained him of vitality. Her fluctuating sympathy may suggest her ambivalence toward Anderson, many of whose personal traits are divided between Vetch and Benham.

A critical tone also exists at times toward both these characters, and it extends as well to the younger male character, Stephen Culpeper, whose romance with the high-spirited (Glasgow-like) Patty Vetch seems doomed because of his mother's possessiveness. (Anderson's closeness to his mother may have been one of the problems with the Glasgow-Anderson romance; Anderson, in fact, remained a bachelor until his death.)[22] Glasgow's dialogue between Stephen Culpeper and his mother illustrates their relationship:

"My dear boy, it is for your own good. I am sure that you know I am not thinking of myself. I may say with truth that I never think of myself."

It was true. She never thought of herself; but he had sometimes wondered what worse things could have happened if she had occasionally done so.

"I know that, Mother," he answered simply.

"I have but one wish in life and that is to see my children happy," she said, with an air of injured dignity which made him feel curiously guilty.

It was the old infallible method, he knew. She would never yield her point; she would never relax her pressure; she would never admit defeat until he married another woman.

"I want nobody else in your place, Mother." [23]

Throughout *One Man in His Time*, Glasgow draws unsatisfying male characters. Even though they may voice the same philosophies that seemed convincing in Blackburn's tones in *The Builders*, Glasgow undercuts their effect by creating the competition between Vetch and Benham—and by giving most of her attention to one of her most powerful heroines. Not incidentally, the heroine of *One Man in His Time* is one of Glasgow's oldest. Caroline Meade of *The Builders* was an unremarkable thirty-two; Corinna Page of this novel is a charming, beautiful forty-eight. It is with this character that Glasgow gives us her most complete self-portrait.

The novel takes Corinna (whose exotic name might recall the *Vardah* that Anderson had called Ellen early in their romance) from her opening wistful lament ("She had possessed everything except the one thing she had wanted," 105) through an education which gives her satisfaction without romance. Even at an accomplished forty-eight Corinna defines herself first as a woman without a mate; for all her achievements and friends, she feels her life empty, artificial: "a gray lane without a turning that stretched on into nothingness!" (119). The angst that mars her happiness is prompted by her feelings of superiority—the people around her, the men who might be lovers, are inferior. Whenever she has hoped, she has been disillusioned: "Isn't that life?—sparrows for larks always?" she asks Gideon Vetch.

Disillusioned as she is, Corinna moves with the ageless charm of a truly beautiful, candid woman through a world that recognizes her quality. Her confidence comes from her self-esteem; she understands society and its relationships, and her power comes from working within conventions. She is a beauty; she deserves admiration. Disappointed that Vetch seems disinterested in her, she shows a conscious use of her beauty as she thinks, "Her sense of defeat was humorous rather than resentful; yet she realized that it contained a disagreeable sting. Was her long day over at last? Had the sun set on her conquests? Had her adventurous return to power been merely a prelude to the ultimate Waterloo?" (122). Corinna's grasp of the male psyche is an integral part of her life; she is a woman experienced in love and flirtation. As Corinna muses on her life and on her real disinterest in finding a second husband, Glasgow creates long melodious sentences to describe her solitude before revealing her wry thoughts about the male half of the race:

> The afternoon sunshine streamed through the dull gold curtains into the old print shop where Corinna sat in her tapestry-covered chair between the tea-table and the log fire. . . . The flames made a pleasant whispering sound over the cedar logs; her favourite wide-open creamy roses with golden hearts scented the air; and the delicate China tea in her cup was drawn to perfection. As she lay back in the big chair but one thing disturbed her serenity—and that one thing was within. . . . Men had ceased to interest her because she knew them too well. She knew by heart the very machinery of their existence, the secret mental springs which moved them so mechanically; and she felt to-day that if they had been watches, she could have taken them apart and put them together again without suspending for a minute the monotonous regularity of their works. (142)

Later, as the distinguished Benham realizes that he loves her, she waits, but with little expectancy ("There was no excitement in such things now, she had had too much experience," 152). Once they are engaged, she replies to a friend, "One dreads the lonely fireside as one grows older" (211). This hardly enthusiastic comment is meant to show that the Page-Benham romance is a matter of propriety rather than heart, and probably serves to mask Glasgow's own situation with Anderson. Benham, for all his strengths, is—like Anderson—emotionless. When Corinna sacrifices herself so that Alicia Rokeby can recapture Benham, she is escaping a marriage that would never have been fulfilling. Her characteristic fault had been too great a passion ("So often in the past the older woman had given herself abundantly only to meet disappointment and ingratitude," 157).

In *One Man in His Time*, Corinna remains comforted only by the glimpse of the passion Gideon Vetch might have provided, had he not been killed. As Glasgow tells her story, Corinna Page exists as Corinna Page, never dependent on men. She is rather the giving, generous friend, quick to warn young Patty that a woman must salvage something of herself in any relationship:

Just so much and no more. . . . Give with the mind and the heart;
but keep always one inviolable sanctity of the spirit—of the buried
self beneath the self. (286)

Speaking with the aphorisms familiar to Glasgow's letters and notebooks, Corinna cajoles, "Things will fail . . . if we lean too hard on
them" (291). For all her stoic endurance, however, she feels pain in her
renunciation of Benham:

"I understand," said Corinna, and her voice was scarcely more
than a breath. Though she did not withdraw the hand that the other
had taken, she looked away from her through the French window,
into the garden where the twilight was like the bloom on a grape.
The fragrance became suddenly intolerable. It seemed to her to be
the scent not only of spring, but of death also, the ghost of all the
sweetness that she had missed. "I shall never be able to bear the
smell of spring again in my life," she thought. (295)

As she talks with Alicia, deciding to renounce Benham for this woman
who has no life aside from her love for him, Corinna adds image to image in the accumulation of her painful recognition.

There was pain, which was less pain than a great sadness; and there
was the thought that she was very lonely; that she must always be
lonely. Many thoughts passed through her mind; but beyond them,
stretching far away into the future, she saw her own life like a deserted road filled with dead leaves and the sound of distant voices
that went by. (295)

For Glasgow, those half-heard, distant voices are as much a personal
image of isolation as they are a rhetorical one; and the desiccation of the
leafy road also bespeaks her poignant sense of loss. The description becomes even more personal as she continues, "She could never find rest,
she knew. Rest was the one thing that had been denied her—rest and
love." Sleeplessness, anxiety, depression—Glasgow's life was a battle,
as we have seen, with the dispirited symptoms for which there are few
cures. But out of this vacuum, this deprivation, comes—for Corinna
and, one assumes, for Glasgow—the fortitude: "Her destiny was the
destiny of the strong who must give until they have nothing left, until
their souls are stripped bare": Glasgow's "vein of iron."

Glasgow's ability to present Corinna as both passionate and philosophical, suffering yet enduring, is the real accomplishment of *One Man in His Time*. That she becomes overly didactic with this character mars the novel somewhat, but her need to be explicit reinforces Corinna's importance as author surrogate. Glasgow too is forty-eight, charming, envied, a woman who has known success and love, and a woman who fears the lonely future.

Contrary to the title, Corinna Page is central to the novel; the male characters—Vetch, Benham, Culpeper—only divide the focus of attention. Vetch is the low-born idealist, achieving political power not out of personal aim but rather for the people. He most closely resembles Blackburn, but in this novel, Benham as well as Vetch reflects Anderson. Both Benham and Culpeper are of good Virginia stock, Benham representing the proper conservative element, and Culpeper the younger opportunity to change. Benham too is an idealist who delights in abstractions; he has presumably been defeated by Vetch because his language shows his lack of concern for the people. Glasgow shows Benham's deficiency in emotion during the parting scene with Corinna, as she points to his "temperamental inability to call things by their right names." His lack of feeling for people brings Corinna to the realization that

> they did not speak the same language. She felt that she had struck against something as dry and cold and impersonal as an abstract principle. A ludicrous premonition assailed her that in a little while he would begin to talk about his public duty (303–304)

as Blackburn had. Glasgow's opinion of political rhetoric as a personal mode of expression becomes clear in these novels.

The melodramatic plot of Patty Vetch's parentage seems chosen to emphasize that difference between Benham and Vetch. Benham cannot even sense the pain he has caused his former lover, a woman who has divorced her husband for him, while Vetch has taken on the responsibility of rearing a strange infant about whom he knows nothing because her mother—also a stranger to him—is being jailed. One man cannot understand human need; the other cannot help but respond to it. Glasgow's indictment is apparent.

For all this novel's contrivance, however, it maintains reader interest more easily than had *The Builders*. Though both propound a surfeit of turgid political philosophy, in *The Builders* all characters ascribe to the beliefs voiced. Blackburn seldom speaks anything but ideology, and Caroline Meade echoes him more often than she speaks any sentiments of her own. Her aspirations are as dull as her life:

She had not wanted colour; she had attuned her life to grey days and quiet backgrounds, and the stark forms of things that were without warmth or life. (371)

Caroline is herself a creature of sacrifice as much as was Virginia Pendleton. In *One Man in His Time*, however, Glasgow has found a language to counter the political dialogues: Corinna's voice cuts through the rhetoric, as do the voices of Vetch and Patty. Idealism here, of at least one sort, is conveyed best through action.

For all the obvious differences in these two novels, it is interesting that both have been considered inferior, of importance primarily for their portrayals of the Henry Anderson character. Reviewers and critics have paid little attention to the women characters,[24] although it seems clear that Glasgow was at least as interested in portraying Caroline Meade and Corinna Page as she was in characterizing Anderson. Locked into the relationship with him as she was—through a complex set of circumstances—she could not very easily exclude him, or male characters that resembled him, from her current work. For Glasgow as writer, the greatest gift she could give to the man she attempted to love was a novel written for/about/in honor of him. David Blackburn in *The Builders* will assuredly live as high tribute to Glasgow's conception of Anderson during the early years of their engagement. Motivated only by ideals, as unfit to live in the world of pomp and villainy as a child, Blackburn renounces his only chance for happiness in giving up Caroline; Caroline, conveniently and predictably, understands. She knows he believes in his ideals and cannot see past them; she trusts his superior intellect. As a result she faces her lonely life—as poor as it is isolated—with equanimity. Blackburn may be a fool, but he is a financially comfortable one.

Glasgow's tendency to deify such martyrdom is no longer present, however, in *One Man in His Time*, and in her change of emphasis from the self-sacrificing Caroline to the self-possessed Corinna she presents a different set of values. The other characters she was creating during the years of the post-*Virginia* period, featured largely in the short stories which she had seldom (to this point) written, were female and equally independent, and were often paired with male characters who were either vapid and insensitive, or downright traitorous.

For all Glasgow's earlier reticence about focusing on women protagonists, she draws a variety of effective female characters in her stories. As Richard K. Meeker points out in his introduction to the collected stories, many of these women prefigure characters from the later novels.[25] Perhaps more significant at this period of Glasgow's career, the stories gave her a means of drawing numerous different women. Many of these female characters were quite changed from her earlier protagonists, and, accordingly, served as exploration for some characters who might meet the cultural obstacles with those more "indirect" methods of which she had spoken in 1916, those of "indirect influence or subtlety." [26] By this stage in her life, Glasgow had learned that any woman's ability to make successful choices, like that of the artist, was crucial. She had also learned that pleasing herself and pleasing a reading audience was not always possible. If some readers would idealize the Virginias, and feminists demand the Gabriellas, Glasgow knew too well that somewhere between them lived a whole gamut of American women.

In both Glasgow's earliest story, the 1897 "Between Two Shores," and one of her most powerful, the 1917 "Thinking Makes It So," she explores several standard plots for the adventurous turn-of-the-century woman. In "Between Two Shores," Lucy Smith comes to love a shipboard stranger and saves him from arrest for some mysterious past crime. Her "love," consuming and physically powerful, is thus capable of changing lives. The cultural assumption is clear—the best use of *her* life is to save the life of her beloved, a man, and a criminal at that. Margaret French, the forty-three-year-old unmarried poet of "Thinking Makes It So," finds an equally romantic fulfillment. When the unknown John Brown writes to her praising her poems, her physical appearance begins to change; she dresses in an atypical "flaming rose color" and is transformed into a striking woman. This paean to the power of the imagination ends with the meeting of the lovers and gives Glasgow another story in the Cinderella tradition. That Margaret is a middle-aged writer waiting to be brought to life through a man's love suggests Glasgow's personal situation in 1917, when she had just become engaged to Anderson.

Most of Glasgow's stories, however, feature the defiantly strong women protagonists rather than any implementation of conventional plot. In fact, even her four stories billed as "ghost tales"—the ostensible reason for her move into short fiction—are as much character studies of female protagonists as they are suspense stories. Lucy Dare, who betrays her Northern lover to the Confederacy in "Dare's Gift," and Mrs. Vanderbridge, who bests her spirit rival in "The Past," are women who experience spiritual awakening or recognition and act on it: "I had to do it. I would do it again," affirms Lucy Dare.[27] It is most often the

women characters who perceive the essential situations. Women characters can apprehend the spirits in the ghost tales because of their uncriti-
cal sympathy, their willingness to respond to needs, whether or not human. As Glasgow presents these characters, their clairvoyance is a
consistently positive ability. They are not charlatans.

Throughout her stories, Glasgow sets insensitive men against more
perceptive women, and what begins as a simple narrative tactic grows
into theme. "The Difference" is an effective story about a happily married woman who receives a letter from her husband's mistress. Ready to
relinquish him after hearing the impassioned description of their love
from Rose Morrison, the wife Margaret is both surprised and disappointed to hear her husband term the affair only "recreation":

> Recreation! The memory of Rose Morrison's extravagant passion
> smote her sharply. How glorified the incident had appeared in the
> girl's imagination, how cheap and tawdry it was in reality. A con-
> tinual compromise with the second best, an inevitable surrender to
> the average, was this the history of all romantic emotion? For an
> instant, such is the perversity of fate, it seemed to the wife that she
> and this strange girl were united by some secret bond which George
> could not share—by the bond of woman's immemorial disil-
> lusionment. (183)

Man's consistent ability to disappoint becomes a pervasive theme in
Glasgow's later fiction; not only Corinna Page experiences disillusionment. The dichotomy of woman's moral supremacy and man's inept-
ness seems to be evinced in more than their sexual roles; Glasgow has
defined the differences in the capacity to love as being intimately con-
nected with the imaginative life of the characters. As Margaret's wise
friend had said,

> When a man and a woman talk of love they speak two different
> languages. . . . women love with their imagination and men with
> their senses. (170)

Once Glasgow had made this statement of "The Difference" so force-
fully, she concentrated on stories that emphasize the foibles of the self-
centered acquisitive male and the women who relate (love, make excuses for, live in deference to, etc.) to him. "Doesn't everything come
back to the men?" asks the wry Geraldine Plummer in "The Artless
Age." She has changed herself chameleon-like to capture and marry

Richard Askew. Geraldine is, however, in control; she may have set her ambition too low but her aim is clear. She marries Richard, against incredible odds, but she knows what she has gotten.

Self-understanding is the strength of Mrs. Kenton as well in "Romance and Sally Byrd." One of Glasgow's most bitter stories, this one narrates the scene between the faithful wife—whose only role in life is to welcome her philandering husband back after each escapade—and the young, would-be mistress.

> Mrs. Kenton's face softened. "How old are you?"
> "Nineteen. Or I was when I came here."
> The other smiled. "At nineteen nothing is permanent. You will forget him and be happy."
> Sally Byrd shook her head. "I shall forget, but I shall not be happy. It has broken my heart."
> A wistful expression crossed the other's face. "No, your heart isn't broken—not so long as it hurts. When your heart is really broken, it lies still and dead like mine. You can't imagine the relief it is," she added simply, "to have your heart break at last." (233)

Relief it might have been, but by 1924 Glasgow was viewing experience as more necessary to maturity than disillusioning. Most of her attention during the mid-twenties was going to that wisest of her female protagonists, Dorinda Oakley, but she was not above choosing less experienced women as protagonists for her stories.

The pathetic if successful Judith Campbell, for example, in "The Professional Instinct," makes the mistake of believing that Professor John Estbridge can share her self-abnegating passion. When she has been offered a prestigious academic position and is about to leave the area, the married but flirtatious Estbridge asks,

> "Judith, would you give it up if I asked you?"
> "If you asked me?"
> "Would you stay—would you give it up if I asked you?" The glow in her face seemed to pervade her whole body while she stood before him transfigured.
> "I would give up the whole world if you asked me."
> "You would sacrifice your ambition—your future?"
> A laugh broke from her lips. "I haven't any ambition—any future—except yours." (248)

It is this passion that Glasgow so admires, but it is its misdirection that she so often laments. As William Kelly concludes, these stories show Glasgow in her greatest period of experimentation, working with "ideas which would be incorporated into her best later books."[28] Kelly sees strong parallels between *Barren Ground*, for example, and "Jordan's End," in which the Antigone-like wife murders her husband, defying all convention and creating her own personal bereavement: "Suddenly, without the warning of a sob, a cry of despair went out of her, as if it were torn from her breast. 'He was my life,' she cried, 'and I must go on!'" (215). Woman alone with only land, place, responsibility, sorrow—Judith prefigures Dorinda Oakley's situation, but the more startling parallels between the 1923 story and the 1925 novel are in the way Glasgow describes nature to image character's feelings. Jordan's death is discovered on an "ashen" November day, the somberness of which permeates the entire story.

> In the middle of the lawn, where the trees had been stripped bare in the night, and the leaves were piled in long mounds like double graves, she stopped and looked in my face. The air was so still that the whole place might have been in a trance or asleep. Not a branch moved, not a leaf rustled on the ground, not a sparrow twittered in the ivy; and even the few sheep stood motionless, as if they were under a spell. Farther away, beyond the sea of broomsedge, where no wind stirred, I saw the flat desolation of the landscape. (214–15)

Making description work more intensely as part of both plot and characterization gave Glasgow a powerful method of creating more nuance of personality. Dorinda Oakley, as character, could only benefit from Glasgow's discoveries.

CHAPTER 5

Finding Options

There she stood, her orange-colored shawl bravely lighting the broom-sedge-smothered land: "Bare, starved, desolate, the country closed in about her."[1] With a very slim chance for happiness, Dorinda Oakley still managed to look, in Glasgow's loving opening scene, "as if she were running toward life." The exemplification of Glasgow's stubborn "I will not be defeated,"[2] Dorinda is like Glasgow's earlier heroines in that she is searching, questing, impatient of roles and society's expectations. She flees not only from the humdrum poverty of Pedlar's Mill; she also resents the near-slavery of having to be a wife in such poverty.

> Her nature, starved for emotional realities, and nourished on the gossamer substance of literature, found its only escape in the fabrication of dreams. Though she had never defined the sensation in words, there were moments when it seemed to her that her inner life was merely a hidden field in the landscape, neglected, monotonous, abandoned to solitude, and yet with a smothered fire, like the wild grass, running through it. At twenty, her imagination was enkindled by the ardour that makes a woman fall in love with a religion or an idea. (12)

Dorinda hungered for "adventure, happiness, even unhappiness, if it were only different" (12).

A creature of passion, Dorinda Oakley loves Jason Greylock passionately; she comes to love the land with an equal passion. The latter affection, however, is a prize she must learn to savor. The path of Dorinda's education, for all her stubborn independence, parallels that of Virginia Pendleton: Dorinda longs for romantic love; she gives all to her infatuation for Jason. And even though she questions the sterility of the lives of her self-sacrificing mother and her dying friend, Rose Emily Pedlar ("Dorinda sighed. Was this life? 'I don't see how you keep it up, Ma,' she said, with weary compassion," 49), she admires these women. She reacts against their "morbid unselfishness," but she does turn to them when she wants answers to her questions about love and marriage.

By 1925 Glasgow had become aware that a woman's only accurate information would come from another woman.

Contrasted with the dialogue about marriage between Virginia Pendleton and her mother in the 1913 *Virginia*, Dorinda's exchange with her mother about that subject is a bleak deflation of any notion of "romance." Mrs. Oakley minces no words:

> Grandfather used to say that when a woman got ready to fall in love the man didn't matter, because she could drape her feeling over a scarecrow and pretend he was handsome. . . . The way I've worked it out is that with most women, when it seems pure foolishness, it ain't really that. It's just the struggle to get away from things as they are. (103)

To emphasize the accuracy of Mrs. Oakley's comment, Glasgow underlines it by showing Dorinda's surprised chagrin: "To get away from things as they are! Was this all there was in her feeling for Jason; the struggle to escape from the endless captivity of things as they are? In the bleak dawn of reason her dreams withered like flowers that are blighted by frost."

It is important that the stunting of Dorinda's romantic dreams occurs here, long before she knows she has been betrayed. Dorinda's real betrayal is more than Jason's abandonment; it is as ageless as history, and stems from parents' failures to create lives of promise for their daughters. When Dorinda questions her mother further, Mrs. Oakley speaks directly to the point of self-actualization—feminine independence:

> "Marriage is the Lord's own institution, and I s'pose it's a good thing as far as it goes. Only," she added wisely, "it ain't ever going as far as most women try to make it. You'll be all right married, daughter, if you just make up your mind that whatever happens, you ain't going to let any man spoil your life." (103)

The tendency of women to let their lives be shaped, damaged, and even destroyed by their husbands (fathers, sons) is so common that Mrs. Oakley does not elaborate on it. Yet one of the ironies of *Barren Ground* is that after burying her own gentle if ineffectual husband, Mrs. Oakley *does* allow her life to be destroyed by her careless younger son, Rufus. When Rufus is accused of murder, Mrs. Oakley perjures herself to give him an alibi.

"Rufus was right here with me the whole evening."

When she had finished speaking, she reached for a chair and sat down suddenly, as if her legs had failed her. Rufus broke into a nervous laugh which had an indecent sound, Dorinda thought, and Mr. Wigfall heaved a loud sigh of relief.

"Well, you jest come over tomorrow and tell that to the magistrate," he said effusively. "I don't reckon there could be a better witness of anybody. Thar ain't nobody round Pedlar's Mill that would be likely to dispute yo' word." (313)

Mrs. Oakley never recovers from the shock of Rufus' crime, and from her own betrayal of basic moral values. Her love for her son has cost her both integrity and life.

Dorinda's reaction to her mother's sacrifice shows a great deal about Glasgow's view of the role of woman, and especially of mother. " 'I couldn't have done it,' " Dorinda thinks, judging the act a waste; "She was shocked; she was unsympathetic; she was curiously exasperated. Her mother's attitude to Rufus impressed her as sentimental rather than unselfish; and she saw in this painful occurrence merely one of the first fruits of that long weakness. . . . 'I'm not made that way,' " Dorinda decided. " 'There's something deep down in me that I value more than love or happiness or anything outside myself' " (316). Glasgow implies that healthful relationships will provide choices for children, not excuses. She would undoubtedly agree with Adrienne Rich, writing in 1974 in *Of Woman Born*,

The most important thing one woman can do for another is to illuminate and expand her sense of actual possibilities. . . . *To refuse to be a victim.* . . . As daughters we need mothers who want their freedom and ours.[3]

In her first dozen novels, Glasgow had yet to create that kind of mother.

The primary story line of *Barren Ground*, which is the account of Dorinda's life after Jason has jilted her, illustrates the scarcity of options for women intent on getting away from things as they are. It also brings Dorinda into frequent contrast with her mother, so that as she develops strength after strength, Mrs. Oakley fades more and more indistinguishably into the background. "There were times when it seemed to Dorinda that she could not breathe within the stark limitations of her mother's point of view" (298). Dorinda's eventual triumph may have resulted as much from the conflict with her mother as from her own vein of iron—or so the structure of the novel suggests.

In *Barren Ground*, Glasgow successfully breaks down the stereotypes of "romance." As a betrayed woman carrying an illegitimate child, Dorinda should seek either forgiveness or vengeance. Narrowly missing the opportunity for the latter, she does neither; instead she looks for a new kind of life. She uses her talent in ways her culture finds scandalous—for a woman. Wearing borrowed overalls, funded with borrowed money, Dorinda withdraws from the society that would shame her to regain her reputation in the man's world of farming. (Dorinda is, in a sense, regaining her family's reputation as well; the land had been in her mother's family and her father had been able to do little but lose what soil had been tillable. Reclaiming the land is a responsibility of the matriarchal line, in one sense.) Only when Dorinda has been successful does she return to wearing women's clothes and to attending the church that would have banished her during her pregnancy.

Although she has dressed as a man during these ten years of struggle, Dorinda has not become masculine. She is still a handsome woman, caring for Nathan Pedlar's children and remaining loyal to Fluvanna, who works with her on the farm. Indeed, it is Fluvanna's discovery that Dorinda has developed crow's-feet that sends her to the dressmaker for her first church dress in a decade.

For all its dedication, Dorinda's life after Jason's betrayal is not exemplary, however, for much of it is prompted by bitterness.[4] Glasgow shows clearly that fear and resentment have tempered Dorinda's insistence that work is all-important. It takes many more years before she learns the compassion that marks her as a woman. Glasgow's story in *Barren Ground* is not only an account of the way a woman learns to know the land or the culture but also the more important story of the way a woman learns to know herself.

What is most masterful in this novel, contrasted with *Virginia*, *Life and Gabriella*, and *One Man in His Time*, is that Glasgow conveys her theme through a subtle overlay of imagery most appropriate to Dorinda's absorption in the land and its vegetation. The whole novel hinges upon the reader's definition of the word "barren," and various levels of irony. Childless as she is, Dorinda herself might be termed *barren*, but Glasgow shows clearly that Dorinda has never been a barren woman: she has known passion, she has conceived. And what she wrests from the generally unyielding land is fruit, success, promise for the future—the opposite of barrenness. The title phrase is used in this way early in the novel:

Almost everybody is poor at Pedlar's Mill. The Ellgoods are the only people who have prospered. The rest of us have had to wring whatever we've had out of barren ground. (231)

"That's what life is for most people, I reckon. . . . Just barren ground where they have to struggle to make anything grow," Dorinda observes as she runs away to New York, pregnant and frightened but determined not to accept her culture's judgment (190).

In *Barren Ground*, Glasgow uses the land and the kind of growth it supports as an index to the kind of characters involved in its farming. The chaos and filth of the Greylocks' place is more sinister than the omnipresent blur of the broomsedge, although that too is frightening in its commonplace wildness. "Wave by wave, that symbol of desolation encroached in a glimmering tide on the darkened boundaries of Old Farm. It was the one growth in the landscape that thrived on barrenness; the solitary life that possessed an inexhaustible vitality" (125). In the opening section of the novel, Glasgow compares the lineage of her Scotch-Irish mother to the pines, and that of the low-born Virginians to the broomsedge (8). Broomsedge contributed nothing.

Throughout the novel, land is adversary, never comforter. Part of Dorinda's success in her battle with that land stems from the vein of iron that runs through her character—an image Glasgow creates to undercut the strength of the land. Caught against the unyielding earth, Dorinda met the forces that might have conquered her with her own persistent strength: "The vein of iron in her nature would never bend, would never break, would never disintegrate in the furnace of emotion" (170); "Deep down in her, beneath the rough texture of experience, her essential self was still superior to her folly and ignorance. . . . she was not broken. She could never be broken while the vein of iron held in her soul" (180). Dorinda is unique in this strength; Glasgow has shown the ruin of the inarticulate Josiah, the devastation of Rose Emily and Mrs. Oakley, the victimization of the Greylocks. Only Nathan Pedlar, the Ellgood men, and Dorinda succeed, perhaps because they understand the power of the land and the necessity of controlling it. Once Dorinda accepts her duty to the land, she can be receptive when Old Matthew admonishes her, "Put yo' heart in the land. The land is the only thing that will stay by you" (323).

The land—rather, her power over it—becomes Dorinda's center. Glasgow structures the novel to emphasize the stages of power in Dorinda's life. Part one, "The Broomsedge," shows the striking if flighty romantic girl, wearing her orange shawl and determined to find some beauty in life by the easy route of escape through sensual excitement. Glasgow uses the life of Jason's bride, Geneva Ellgood Greylock, to contrast that of her heroine: Geneva's use of coercion and duplicity to marry Jason; her disappointment when the marriage fails and there are no children; her insanity when this single source of meaning in her life crumbles. Geneva's tragedy as a woman is that she has never come to know what Dorinda understands early, that life has some value "as long as she could rule her own mind" (250).

This understanding comes to Dorinda during part two, "Pine," when Pa's uncomplaining acceptance of death parallels his stoic attention to the hardy pine outside his window. Emblematic of his own struggle to exist, the tree has somehow grown from the impoverished land: it shows tenacity, fortitude, the ability to thrive. In this section too Glasgow stresses that the land's barrenness is innate: underproductivity is due to not only poor farming tactics but also the physical poverty of the land. The desolation of the land and people throughout the novel sets the tone for Glasgow's Hardy-like conditioning. When Mrs. Oakley describes women's search for husbands as "just the struggle to get away from things as they are," she catches exactly the temper of endurance in the midst of desolation. And as Dorinda comes to develop such traits as strength and perseverance, she recognizes that her father too has had strength. He has been like the pine, whereas Jason in his weakness was like the prickly purple thistle, only obstructing her plow and her life (240). In the midst of her struggle to bury Jason, during her dream of thistles with Jason's face on them, she is joined to the imagery of her father (pine) and herself (life-everlasting): "Was it only her imagination, or did the wind, blowing over the city, bring the fragrance of pine and life-everlasting?" (240).

Part three, titled "Life-Everlasting," brings Dorinda to the knowledge of joy through complete dedication: "For the next few years she gave herself completely to Five Oaks. Only by giving herself completely, only by enriching the land with her abundant vitality, could she hope to restore the farm" (397). But her dedication has the ulterior motive of settling the score with Jason and the Greylock family, too weak to handle Five Oaks on its own terms; and it is not until she has lost her husband, Nathan Pedlar, and has come to realize that the ruined Jason remembers nothing of their early passion that she finally does accept the reality of her life of service. Dorinda's reward—for her life of affirmation and deprivation—is not fairy-tale happiness, at least not in *Barren Ground*, but a kind of constancy, a satisfaction with herself which is also a self-abnegation without martyrdom. Dorinda's relationships with the people of Pedlar's Mill and with Nathan's children please her; her love for her land continues strong and beautiful. "Though in a measure destiny had defeated her, for it had given her none of the gifts she had asked of it, still her failure was one of those defeats, she realized, which are victories. At middle age, she faced the future without romantic glamour, but she faced it with integrity of vision. The best of life, she told herself with clear-eyed wisdom, was ahead of her" (510). Dorinda's view of the future was hopeful because she had grown to accept the life that suited her. As she had predicted in New York, she would learn to fill her years "with something better than broomsedge. That's the first thing that puts out on barren soil, just broomsedge. Then that goes and pines come to stay—pines and life-everlasting" (233).

Glasgow's use of the three-part structure, suggestively but not didactically titled, enriches the force of *Barren Ground* immeasurably. Worksheets for the novel in draft show that she had once titled the three divisions "Sowing," "Locust Years," and "The Harvest."[5] Without knowing exactly how she had divided the novel at this stage, the reader cannot gloss her use of "locust years." The titles as chosen in this draft are much more limiting, however, and much more moralistic than those of the final version. At another point in Glasgow's work on *Barren Ground*, she had divided it into five sections which were labeled with both seasonal designations and those of vegetation:

1. The End of Winter (Broomsedge)
2. Spring (Pine)
3. Summer (Life-Everlasting)
4. Autumn
5. The Return of Winter

Although Glasgow is careful to place the opening chapter at the end of winter, the other sections are less dependent on season. The tone achieved by adding "Autumn" and "The Return of Winter" to the three constant titles is clearly less than affirmative. Once Glasgow was into the writing, once she had, indeed, used the process of writing as an exploration, Glasgow saw that the impact of this novel had to be positive. Readers were too quick to assume that any unmarried woman was suspect;[6] Dorinda's life of self-fulfillment would never be seen as satisfying unless Glasgow kept reinforcing that view.

The place of *Barren Ground* in the Glasgow canon parallels that of

The Builders, and Dorinda's choice of lifestyle echoes that of David Blackburn—only, blessedly, without Blackburn's rhetoric. The characters of Blackburn and Oakley represent Glasgow's belief in the selfless life of altruism. Just as a man was likely to move from what might appear to be the grossest materialism in order to give his attention to idealistic pursuits, so a mature woman could move from an obsession with romantic love to an enjoyment of nonpersonal giving. She would become unself-conscious; she would look past her personal comfort and pleasure to larger giving. While Glasgow had implied this kind of progression within the character of Caroline Meade in *The Builders*, the force of the woman's philosophy in that book is dulled (if not buried) beside Blackburn's eloquence. With Dorinda in *Barren Ground*, Glasgow has only the woman's position to stress, and she does it well.

Perhaps Glasgow did not realize fully what she had achieved until *Barren Ground* was finished, although her comments to Hugh Walpole in 1923 suggest that she did know how important this book would be to her reputation. *Barren Ground* remained her favorite novel, for in it she had learned to break away from the conventions of both the romance and the novel of manners in order to write the story demanding voice: "Dorinda was free, while the theme was still undeveloped, to grow, to change, to work out her own destiny."[7] "It is the best book I have written"; "the one of my books I like best"; "putting my whole heart into a book in which I believe"—Glasgow's enthusiasm for the novel never diminished; in 1932 she spoke again of her love for the novel:

> In reading this book over again, after seven years, I felt, as I had felt when I was writing it, that it is the truest novel ever written. Not true to a locality only—I don't mean that—but to life and to the inevitable change and fall of the years. That book deserves to live. It is a perfectly honest interpretation of experience, without illusion, without evasion.[8]

The similarities in Dorinda's relinquishing her need for romance and Glasgow's bitter struggle against full dependence on Henry Anderson, whether through marriage or engagement or friendship, are striking. Glasgow acknowledged that the roots for the novel and the character of Dorinda grew from that relationship; as she said in 1928, "A novel like that grows slowly. For ten years I carried that idea in my mind, and I gave three years to the actual writing."[9] Her statements about the Anderson engagement, and its end, in *The Woman Within* also parallel the kind of resolution Dorinda was able to achieve:

Nothing, apparently, had changed—nothing, except that I was free. The obscure instinct that had warned me, in my early life, against marriage, was a sound instinct. . . . I was free from chains. I belonged to myself. . . . After more than twenty-one years, I was at last free. If falling in love could be bliss, I discovered, presently, that falling out of love could be blissful tranquillity. I had walked from a narrow overheated place out into the bracing autumnal colors. People and objects resumed their natural proportions. . . . Gradually, as this grasp weakened and relaxed, all the other parts of my nature, all that was vital and constructive, returned to life. Creative energy flooded my mind, and I felt, with some infallible intuition, that my best work was ahead of me. I wrote *Barren Ground*, and immediately I knew I had found myself.[10]

In Glasgow's preface, she admits to *Barren Ground* being for her a "vehicle of liberation": "After years of tragedy and the sense of defeat that tragedy breeds in the mind, I had won my way to the other side of the wilderness, and had discovered, with astonishment, that I was another and a very different person" (v).

The freedom of finding herself a new woman—less the rebellious child of the solid Glasgow family, more the distinguished and still imaginatively passionate novelist—seemed to give Glasgow a full range of fictional power. Instead of creating character through abstract and philosophical dialogue, Glasgow here turned to concrete descriptions of emotions in play—anger, fear, joy, despair.

It isn't true. It isn't true. The pendulum was swinging more slowly, and suddenly the ticking stopped, and then went on in jerks like a clock that is running down. *It isn't true—true—true.*

She felt cold and wet. Though she had not lost the faculty of recollection, she was outside time and space, suspended in ultimate darkness. There was an abyss around her, and through this abyss wind was blowing, black wind, which made no sound because it was sweeping through nothingness. She lay flat in this vacancy, yet she did not fall through it because she also was nothing. Only her hands, which clutched woodmould, were alive. There was mould under her finger-nails, and the smell of wet earth filled her nostrils. Everything within her had stopped. The clock no longer ticked; it had run down. She could not think, or, if she thought, her thoughts were beyond her consciousness, skimming like shadows over a frozen lake. Only the surface of her could feel, only her skin, and this felt as if it would never be warm again. (155–56)

Glasgow's description of Dorinda's forcing herself to face the reality of Jason's marriage to Geneva is effective because of both the incantatory rhythm and the repetition. The words *abyss, wind, mould, nothing* (and other negatives) occur in a pattern which links the more obvious refrain *It isn't true*, and not even the staccato pace can alleviate the intensity of Dorinda's lament. This passage, and others that are as striking, suggest the accuracy of Glasgow's recollection nearly twenty years later that this novel was "torn out of" herself.[11]

The passage also illustrates Glasgow's growing awareness of the control she could exercise over words, sentences, paragraphs. Stylistically as well as thematically, there is reason to consider *Barren Ground* the beginning of Glasgow's great period. What she achieves in her next three novels—the ironic trilogy of manners that continues her gallery of self-directed, purposeful, and newly tolerant women—is impressive largely because she has developed the control to lure readers into the books: the pace, the identification, the eventual realization is entirely Glasgow's. In learning to rely on herself and her craft—to choose characters and themes and then to shape the fiction to best portray its content—Glasgow had found freedom from as many literary conventions as she had personal ones.

In 1925, Dorinda Oakley "finished with all that" (the legendary romance of a woman's life) in order to find self-fulfilling directions for her healthy existence. In 1925, Ellen Glasgow finished with all that (the legendary romance of every woman's life) in order to find self-fulfilling directions for her healthy existence as writer:

> I wanted "a room of my own," and it was granted me. I wanted a pursuit that I might follow with interest between the cradle and the grave and that, too, was allowed. . . . If I have missed many of the external rewards of success, I have never lost the outward peace and the inward compensation that comes from doing the work one wishes to do.[12]

Glasgow's art, and perhaps her life, show very clearly that there is more than one way of escaping bare and desolate country, and more than one means of "running toward life."

CHAPTER 6

Of Manners, Morals, and Men

Just one year after *Barren Ground*, Glasgow published *The Romantic Comedians*. The short interval between novels surprised her readers, as did the wit and irony of the later novel. *The Romantic Comedians* was a departure for Glasgow, perhaps a necessary one; she later claimed that it was written "for my private diversion." [1] In *Barren Ground* she had treated proud woman as survivor and man as betrayer with such intensity that the three years of writing drained her emotionally. In *The Romantic Comedians*, "a tragicomedy of a happiness-hunter," the Anderson figure (Judge Honeywell) is mocked rather than villainized. Honeywell benefited from Glasgow's "infusion of satire"; [2] he would not have stood the kind of psychological scrutiny Glasgow had provided for Dorinda Oakley. The difference in purpose between the 1925 novel (to create believable character) and the 1926 tragicomedy (to depict society) allowed Glasgow to prove her technical range. As she recalled in *The Woman Within*,

> *Barren Ground* left me drained, but only in one capacity. Immediately, my imagination reacted from the novel of character into the mood of polite comedy. It required three comedies of manners to exhaust this impulse toward ironic humor, and not one of these books betrays, I think, the slightest sign that I had burned up my energy. (275–76)

What Glasgow attempted in her so-called trilogy of manners (*The Romantic Comedians*, 1926; *They Stooped to Folly*, 1929; and *The Sheltered Life*, 1932) was a prolegomena of the foibles of women and men (chiefly the latter) attempting the varieties—and vagaries—of romance. That some of her motivation was bitterness at the foolish behavior of Henry Anderson, rumored during his later years to be courting younger women, is obvious. [3] More of her interest during these years, however—given the success she had achieved in *Barren Ground*, as both novel and renunciation of storybook romance—lay in observing the cyclic and recurring patterns of romantic attraction. Regardless of age, for example, people responded uniformly to spring's dangerous liberation. *The Romantic Comedians* opens with Judge Gamaliel Bland Honeywell arranging lilies on his former wife's grave, surprised at the physical zest he felt after his year of mourning:

> "I am a bird with a broken wing," he sighed to himself, as he had sighed so often into other ears since the day of his bereavement. And while this classic metaphor was still on his lips, he felt an odd palpitation within the suave Virginian depths of his being, where his broken wing was helplessly trying to flutter.
>
> It is astonishing, he reflected, with the slow but honourable processes of the judicial mind, what Spring can do to one even at sixty-five—even at a young sixty-five, he hastened to remind himself. [4]

What Glasgow catches wryly here is the eternal self-delusion of physical youth. The novel chronicles Honeywell through his courtship of and marriage to the young Annabel Upchurch, the end of that marriage, and his recovery from his deathbed with a new infatuation for an equally young nurse. The simplest of Glasgow's plots, this story is meant to be trifling and even trite, but all too recognizable. Judge Honeywell, for all his position, is a character to chuckle over, not to admire or censure; he is the victim of stereotype, implausible in his predictability. In Glasgow's satire, men are created to pursue lovers; that is their only motivation.

Mr. Virginius Littlepage, hero of *They Stooped to Folly*, parallels Honeywell. Happily married to the regal and loving Victoria, whose name suggests her definite quality as contrasted with his pretentious morality, Littlepage spends much of his waking existence dreaming about a fantasy liaison with Amy Dalrymple, town tramp. Glasgow's thoroughly positive characterization of his wife, however, undermines the comedy of Littlepage's obsession. *They Stooped to Folly* does not hesitate to praise characters who love truly and selflessly; such people as Marmaduke Littlepage, Louisa Goddard, Milly Burden, and Aunt Agatha are treated with tenderness instead of ridicule. They are the seekers, people looking not simply for love but rather for "something worth loving." [5]

The difference between the two novels, *The Romantic Comedians* and *They Stooped to Folly*, is achieved through a change of authorial tone and through much more serious attention to the women characters. The central female figures in the 1926 novel, Amanda Lightfoot and Annabel Upchurch, exist primarily as foils for Honeywell's interest. The pathos of Amanda's fading beauty as an unwed, aging belle reminded readers of the characters of *Virginia*: taught to invest her life in the love of a good man, women like Amanda could only wait to be "fulfilled." As Honeywell thought to himself, "It was . . . pathetic, it was even tragic, that she had never known the complete joy of belonging to some good man" (34). That Amanda waits thirty-seven years until Honeywell is widowed, and then continues to wait through his courtship and re-marriage with a twenty-three-year old, provides genuine pathos. As Glasgow described her, "Serene, unselfish, with the reminiscence of a vanished day in her face and figure, she belonged to that fortunate gen-eration of women who had no need to think, since everything was de-cided for them by the feelings of a lady and the Episcopal Church" (143).

Annabel Upchurch, Honeywell's young bride, is another of Glas-gow's daring youngsters. Spirited and frank, Annabel questions Amanda before she will consider accepting Honeywell's proposal: she will not take another woman's beloved. Because Amanda cannot bring herself to truthfulness and admit that she loves Honeywell, however, Annabel does marry him, but she wearies quickly of the pleasures of wealth and soon runs away with a young lover. Though Honeywell's pain in losing her is presented as genuine, Annabel escapes any real criticism for her flight.

As the book is designed, then, we are given insufficient information to identify with either Amanda or Annabel; and what we are given about Honeywell keeps us from identifying with him. Glasgow's narra-tive strategies keep us from becoming involved with any of these char-acters. Here she is interested in social criticism rather than realism. As she said about the theme of *The Romantic Comedians*, "As for the idea— well, I was worn out with having men write what they know or don't know about dangerous ages in women" (*L.*, 90).

They Stooped to Folly also opens with a recognition of the "migrating impulses" spring sets moving. Despite the fact that part one of the three-part novel is titled "Mr. Littlepage," Glasgow's attention falls most often on Victoria, the dying wife. Her 1929 comment to Carl Van Vechten relates the character of Victoria to her earlier aim, in 1916, of drawing a woman so subtle that she would not offend with aggression, nor would she subordinate herself through passivity:

Victoria is really the figure of the pattern. Yes, she was, indeed, so subtle and difficult that you alone perceived what I meant by her. (*L.*, 98)

Although Victoria dies of an undisclosed heart ailment, her presence in her husband's life is stronger after death than before. He never again thinks of Amy—or of any other woman:

> Crowned, radiant, incomparable, a new Victoria, one whom he had never even imagined, had flowered there, out of the throbbing light of his vision. Nothing in his life, not young love, not marriage, not fatherhood, not religious devotion—none of these emotions had ever plunged so far beneath the shallows of consciousness. . . . For this Victoria in heaven, who resembled the actual Victoria as little as a star resembles a glowworm, had won at last his unalterable fidelity. (250)

If betrayal by a man one loves is the lot of most women—and in this novel alone Milly Burden and Mary Victoria Littlepage are betrayed by the same man, Martin Welding; and Aunt Agatha has lived an isolated spinsterhood because of her early betrayal—then Victoria's complete subjugation of Virginius' wanderlust is worth the melodramatic language Glasgow has used. As the epigraph and title suggest, mere charms and art are little defense against the melancholy and guilt "lovely woman" experiences once she has found "too late that men betray."

Once again, the recurrence of this theme must have its personal root in Glasgow's experiences with men, but perhaps in a less tragic sense than the situation would imply. When each of the betrayed women is considered as a person (and the classic unmarried intellectual, Louisa Goddard, must also be included), the reader finds a wide range of ability and common sense, and even happiness. The simple pleasures of the reclusive Aunt Agatha are above question, and one is reminded of Glasgow's note in the manuscripts that "Aunt Agatha the ruined woman is not only the victim but the invention of man."[6] Given the prevailing social attitude that women are happiest when living in wedlock, part of the impact of Glasgow's trilogy is her frequent portrayal of the happiest women as those living alone, for whatever reason. Milly Burden, in fact, appears to be pining only for the love of Martin. When he asks her to run away with him, however, she refuses, eager to be on her independent way to New York and free from the constraints of living with her mother.

Glasgow explained in the preface of *They Stooped to Folly* that the novel was in part an answer to assumptions often made about women, but was more directly an exploration of the most common myths about women. Discounting the pervasive "woman as inspiration" myth, Glasgow opted for that of the "ruined" woman and promptly wove into the story three different generations of that species—Aunt Agatha, Mrs. Dalrymple, and Milly Burden. "Here was sentiment; here was chivalry; here was moral tradition; here was a well-honoured invention of man."[7] That the novel was dedicated to her friend James Branch Cabell "in acknowledgement of Something About Eve" also suggests that the fiction had sprung from both personal and literary interests. That it had gone past what Glasgow had conceived to be simply "satire" into a "serious study, with ironic overtones, it is true, of contemporary society"[8] is another illustration of her reliance on letting her fiction take its own direction, remaining responsive to needs and sentiments of author as well as characters.

For all Glasgow's intention of featuring "ruined" women, her attention fell largely on Victoria Littlepage. As we have seen, Glasgow is pleased when readers recognize the centrality of that good wife and mother, but even Glasgow herself was surprised at that centrality. As she explains in the preface,

> I had meant to keep Victoria in the background, to draw her, somewhat sketchily and flippantly, as a tiresome good woman. . . . Gradually, as the book progressed, I found myself to be concentrating upon her, and to be trying, through her mind and heart, to explore the depths of the average woman of good will.

The change this emphasis makes to the structure of the book is clear; characters revolve around Victoria and she does become the center. Glasgow also points out in the preface that she was especially happy with drawing the friendship between Louisa and Victoria:

> Although such an association appears to be not uncommon in life, the novelist, since he is usually a man, has found the relationship to be deficient alike in the excitement of sex and the masculine drama of action. But more and more, in the modern world, women are coming to understand their interdependence as human beings.[9]

The last of Glasgow's trilogy novels, *The Sheltered Life*, emphasizes the theme of women's interdependence. The most bitter of these three novels, *The Sheltered Life* studies the privileged innocence of young women in society; the intensity of Glasgow's resentment suggests that she resented her own early education: "The background is that of my girlhood, and the rudiments of the theme must have lain buried somewhere in my consciousness."[10] Glasgow's comments in her preface about the "perpetual flight from reality" that dominated polite Virginia society give credence to the investigations of Ann Douglas, Russel B. Nye, and others, that nineteenth-century American culture saw women as idealizations of certain moral tendencies. Nye quotes the 1844 Boston *Token of Friendship* as describing women as "the luminary that enlightens," a goddess of "domestic fidelity, social cheerfulness, unostentatious hospitality, and moral and religious benevolence."[11] To prepare for this role of paragon, women underwent a special (and unrealistic) education.

In *The Sheltered Life*, Glasgow creates five women characters who have undergone such educations and have been so victimized—the widowed and self-effacing Cora Archbald; her daughter Jenny Blair Archbald, the subject of the instruction within the novel; the plain and therefore unwanted Etta Archbald and her bolder, more attractive sister, Isabella; and the most beautiful woman in Queenborough, Eva Birdsong. Of these five it is Eva, wife of unfaithful George Birdsong, who becomes the epitome of the wasted woman—protection turned to destruction, happiness to tragedy.

Eva Birdsong moves through life behind a perfect smile, never complaining, breaking through to reality only when her health, her life itself, is threatened. Throughout the novel Glasgow frames Eva with admiring eyes—women hang from their windows to watch her walk past, party-goers circle her as she waltzes with George. Eva is beauty, womanliness, perfection—but such an embodiment of ideals can only be unnatural. As young John Welch, her doctor, concludes,

> I honestly believe that she has never drawn a natural breath since she was married. If she dies . . . it will be the long pretense of her life that has killed her.[12]

Society's precepts reach past human endurance. No person could become the ideal that society demands for its women. Eva's tragedy as person is that she has accepted the illusion of woman's suitable role: she has become the perfect wife, only and exclusively the perfect wife. "You will understand still better when you are older," she advises Jenny. "You will know then that a great love doesn't leave room for anything else in a woman's life. It is everything. . . . you can never give up too much for happiness" (55, 57).

Elaborating on themes she had used earlier in *Virginia* and *Barren*

Ground, Glasgow gives her reader not only intellectual realization of the falsity of this stance toward life but a touching depiction of Eva's physical changes as she comes to sound the depths of her own self-imposed hypocrisy. Some eight years later, when she has realized that she has failed in both keeping her husband and in finding herself, she changes that reassurance to admonition:

> Whatever you do, Jenny Blair, never risk all your happiness on a single chance. Always keep something back, if it is only a crumb. Always keep something back for a rainy day. (271)

Only when Eva shoots her husband after she has found him embracing Jenny, her young friend and protégée, does she manage to break out of the stereotype. What remains for her, however, since her entire identity has been as George's wife, is emptiness. Even her vindication becomes loss.

The protagonist of *The Sheltered Life* is not Eva, however, but Jenny Blair. With fine irony, Glasgow depicts Jenny in the opening chapter as the antithesis of the female characters of Alcott's *Little Women*. Jenny will not be another Jo or Meg or Amy; she instead insists on her right to individualism: "I'm different. I'm different. . . . I'm alive, alive, alive, and I'm Jenny Blair Archbald" (3). Unfortunately, Jenny has few achieving women to imitate. When she chooses Eva as her model, she begins the pattern that dooms her. Both irresponsible and naïve, Jenny is also daring, and that quality implicates her on several occasions with George Birdsong—first when she is a child on roller skates, surprising him at the home of his mulatto mistress; later in his garden; and subsequently in the hospital garden. In each of these meetings, Jenny accepts the male duplicity, the double standard: George has relationships with women besides his wife. Like society and her beloved grandfather, General David Archbald, Jenny accepts Birdsong's philandering. The double standard is an accepted part of Queenborough life. Glasgow does an effective job of showing the inevitability of Jenny's attraction to Birdsong: he is the means of her initiation into male-female mysteries, and he is also the object of her unacknowledged desire. Jenny as miniature Eva copies Eva's mistakes as well as her strengths.

The central irony of *The Sheltered Life*, however, does not depend on its female characters at all. In the novel's structure, Glasgow expertly reflects the culture she is dissecting, for the character who holds power (that "lonely spirit" who "represents the tragedy . . . of the civilized man in a world that is not civilized") is David Archbald—Jenny's grandfather, Eva's admirer, and the apparently wise observer of the scene (xviii). General Archbald is also, unfortunately, spokesman supreme for the traditions of the sheltered life. Jenny, in trusting him, is consequently being misdirected at every turn.

It is David Archbald who assigns the women of his family to conventional roles and, by his own conventional behavior, keeps them locked into those roles. When his wife of thirty years dies, he settles comfortably in as head of household, giving up thoughts of remarriage because of these various family "duties." He takes a dog instead of a second wife. Yet we know from the middle section of the book, "The Deep Past," how unhappy his marriage has been. Trapped by the gentlemanly conventions of his day, Archbald had proposed to Erminia after they had been stranded all night in a buggy (Glasgow parallels this situation with Isabella's adventures, but the modern outcome is much different). Before this, in England, he had loved a married woman. This single passion brought him to the edge of daring. When his lover's child became ill on the eve of what was to have been their elopement, however, he gave her up without further effort. Several months later the woman committed suicide. Though Archbald mourned and felt martyred, the responsibility to act was one he never again assumed.

Characteristically, although his admiration for Eva comes near reverence, he never takes any action to improve her life. He loves from afar, excuses her husband's misbehavior, and sanctions the status quo. His feeling for Eva is idealized; in his own statement of that idealization Glasgow once again projects deep irony. Archbald thinks of his past:

> Of one thing alone he was sure,—life would never again melt and mingle into the radiance that was Eva Birdsong. "Personality," he thought being old and sentimental, "could reach no higher." (279)

Archbald never sees that Eva is without personality; she is the epitome of selflessness. And Archbald himself echoes her self-abnegation:

> He had been a good citizen, a successful lawyer, a faithful husband, an indulgent father; he had been, indeed, everything but himself. Always he had fallen into the right pattern; but the centre of the pattern was missing. Once again, the old heartbreaking question returned. Why and what is human personality? (120)

Socially and politically the strongest character in the novel, Archbald could have created change, eased misery. The irony is that his own grandchild, so shaped by his attitudes and admirations, becomes the reason for Eva's final act, George's death. It is Jenny Blair—innocence and youth—who embraces the wayward husband. Instead of averting tragedy, the Archbald family has shaped it.

The conclusion of the novel brings all these strands together consummately. Archbald, bewildered by the murder, thinks first of protecting his Jenny: "It is too much for you, my darling. You had better go home and wait for your mother." And in an aside to John Welch, "Remember how young she is, and how innocent" (291, 292). The blatancy of the closing scene echoes long after the novel ends, with Jenny's childlike excuse, "Oh, Grandfather, I didn't mean anything. . . . I didn't mean anything in the world!" (292).

In *The Sheltered Life*, Glasgow's spokesman is John Welch, the young physician who knows both families well. The author's preface suggests that the novel needed the dual perspectives of youth and age; what Glasgow fails to make clear, however, is that the views of Jenny Blair and General Archbald—though far apart in age—are nearly parallel. For all his experience, Archbald knows scarcely more about life from a woman's perspective than Jenny. Jenny's section of the novel, "The Age of Make-Believe," is little different from her grandfather's. Both believe in proper concern for convention, in woman's role as wife and mother, in woman's dependence on men, and in suffering. John Welch's cynicism acts to correct the assumptions of the Archbalds. Glasgow gives us his statements in sharp, direct language:

> I sometimes think the whole trouble is too much George. George is not a restful person to live with. Nor, for that matter, is romantic love restful. . . . She must have known, too, in her heart at least, that George wasn't worth it. (199)

> She doesn't like to have him about when she is sick. Did you notice how unnatural she became the minute he entered the room?
> He fell in love with her, as you say, because she was an ideal, and she has determined to remain his ideal until the end. (200)

> You wouldn't [understand], not with your sparrow vision. (218)

Welch's directness is one reason Jenny (of the sparrow vision) dislikes him so clearly. His threatening view robs her and her society of complacency. None of the Archbalds or Birdsongs has ever "seen" their lives from Welch's angle. His perspective is accurate, unlovely, and unhopeful; yet at the book's end he compromises his honesty out of charity for Eva, as he explains George's death as "an accident. He shot himself. It was an accident." No woman leading the sheltered life would shoot her protecting husband. The woman who did, however, can only sit "very erect . . . with her fixed smile. . . . Her face was so vacant that her expression and even her features were like wax" (290). Eva's "personality" was now unmasked, and she appeared the empty caricature she had become through years of unnatural living.

Glasgow's final images of the ruin of sheltered lives and impossible ambitions (to be perfect, to be selfless, to exist on love alone) are devastating. George dead, the blood on his lips like that on the bills of his prized dead ducks, remains a grim parody of the returning conqueror, a Southern Agamemnon caught in the trappings of his masculinity. The final deceit of the Archbalds—Jenny's refusal to take blame, the General's refusal to understand—suggests that the Birdsong tragedy has been wasted. Its impact will be only as terror, as inexplicable horror, rather than as indictment of the social system.

When *The Sheltered Life* was published in 1932, Glasgow was approaching sixty. Given that her mother and many of her sisters had died at ages younger than this, and that her own consistently fragile health had made her existence precarious, she doubtless saw the period as one for taking stock. She became more open in her remarks about life and society, as well as her own role in modern America. She traveled abroad more widely and seemed intent on increasing her range of friends. The years from the writing of *Barren Ground* to the publication of *The Sheltered Life* are Glasgow's fifties, surely the most brilliant decade of her achievement as a writer.

And personally, Glasgow's life was evidently very satisfying. As she wrote in *The Woman Within*, "In this later period my life was expanding. Between fifty and sixty I lived perhaps my fullest and richest years" (273). The fears that had dampened her return home in 1916 seem to have been dispelled; there are many new friendships; there are even some letters from admiring men met in New York during these years. One of her last comments in *The Woman Within* about the Henry Anderson romance is that, in 1921, he gave her a most excellent Christmas gift, the Sealyham puppy Jeremy that was to be her companion for the next decade. Although the Anderson letters show that the suppers and friendship continued far past that 1921 date—intermittently to Glasgow's death in 1945, in fact—her fiction seems to show that Anderson more often fills the role of irritant than of participant. All those foolish older men, many of them wearing rimless spectacles and priding themselves on their elegant Anglo-American manners, are surely embryonic caricatures of Anderson.

In writing about being fifty, Glasgow said that her literary accomplishments gave her her primary satisfaction:

> My mind was thronging with ideas. My imagination was more vital and urgent than it had ever been. I felt that a tombstone had been lifted; but, even while I felt this, I knew that my health was lost, and forever. I had never been strong, except in will, and I knew that many of the past twenty years, though not all of them, had been wasted. Yet, in spite of the physical odds against me, I had begun to write my best books in the middle of the nineteen-twenties. After *Barren Ground*, which I had gathered up, as a rich harvest, from the whole of my life, I had written and published two comedies of manners: *The Romantic Comedians* . . . and *They Stooped to Folly*. In the early nineteen-thirties, I wrote *The Sheltered Life* and *Vein of Iron*. As a whole, these five novels represent, I feel, not only the best that was in me, but some of the best work that has been done in American fiction. (270)

In Glasgow's retrospective comments about her work, she always included *The Sheltered Life*, *Barren Ground*, and *The Romantic Comedians* among her favorites. Other lists often included *They Stooped to Folly*, *Virginia*, and the novel which was written immediately after the trilogy, *Vein of Iron* (see chapter seven).[13] Critical reaction to her work from the 1925 *Barren Ground* through *The Sheltered Life* in 1932 was highly favorable, but none of her four novels won any major awards. Glasgow's disappointment in 1932 when T. S. Stribling's *The Store* rather than *The Sheltered Life* won the Pulitzer Prize for Fiction is well documented, and understandable. She felt that her writing had improved markedly, that her craft as well as her thematic reach was much stronger. If her earlier novels had deserved praise—and they had—then to be given no higher praise for what she was accomplishing in her maturity was disappointing. Undoubtedly she took comfort from words like these of Allen Tate's (May 24, 1933):

> The first day I was distressed, the second irritated, and the third positively furious, that T. S. Stribling should have received the Pulitzer award. I need not name the book that should have got it. . . . *The Sheltered Life* is there to make the award ridiculous in the years to come.[14]

From the mid-twenties on, Glasgow wrote often about her writing technique, her changes in method and craft—as if she were newly conscious of herself as artist. Many of her comments seem casual—"*The Romantic Comedians* bubbled out in one year, though it wasn't nearly so easy to write as it appears. Every word in that book (and in *Barren Ground* too) was carefully chosen" (*L.*, 90). However, she strongly emphasizes technique, as when she discusses theme in *The Romantic Comedians*: "But the way it was done, the style of writing, was what I gave most thought to from the first page to the last" (*L.*, 90). The 1938 prefaces give much support to Glasgow's new image of herself as major modern novelist. In 1931, when she wrote to Dan Longwell that she had at last finished *The Sheltered Life*, she says with pride, "One thing I know: this novel is good, more intense than *They Stooped to Folly*, more sympathetic in treatment, and, I think, deeper and richer in substance."[15] She continues to describe her theory of fiction:

> To me, the novel is experience illuminated by imagination; and by the word "experience" I am trying to convey something more than an attitude or a gesture. In *The Sheltered Life*, as in *Barren Ground*, my idea has been to give the scene an added dimension, a universal rhythm, deeper than any material surface.

Whether it was because the novel pleased her, or because she had felt more involved with the process, she also admitted, "Yes, it is true that I have put more of myself into the book."

Just what the relationship was between the author's emotional involvement in writing and the finished piece of work, no observer will ever determine. Because Glasgow herself—after many years of writing and observing the writing process—attributed some strength to her being more deeply involved with her late work, we can hardly discredit the relationship. For what appears today to be an accurate assessment of the quality of *The Sheltered Life*, and of its import to Glasgow's reputation, let us turn to Allen Tate's September 9, 1932, letter to Glasgow. Tate begins by calling the novel

> the most thorough and sustained novel you have written. . . . the most nearly perfect in form. . . . You have taken your subject beyond the province of the novel of manners into the tragic vision. And that explains the fine coherence of the form and point of view: the whole action leads up to the final scene, and we know that the trouble with the Birdsongs is not the Virginian civilization, but the

fundamental flaw in human nature wherever it is found. . . . That seems to me to be the moral of the book—and every book must have a moral, the good moral being the one that ought not really to be stated, but should, like this one, be the action itself—the "moral" is this—that the sheltered life becomes tragic when it is cut off from appropriate action. Not one of your people had access to a kind of action in which their lives could be fulfilled.[16]

While Tate does not draw sexual differentiation, his last comment surely applies more directly to Glasgow's women characters, those fragile and protected victims of the sheltered life whose anger finally erupts into action that cannot be viewed as appropriate by any society.

As Tate recognizes, however, "The whole action leads up to the final scene": no single person—not George Birdsong, not Jenny Archbald, not Eva, and not the Queenborough society—can be given exclusive blame for Eva's murder. The moral degeneracy, the lack of direction depicted in *The Sheltered Life* is a conspiracy; it exists, Glasgow knew, in the world about her. Yet her accumulation of that knowledge had not turned her to moralizing but rather to re-creating, and in that tactic lies the force of this book. It is *Glasgow*'s lament that gives the novel its anguish; it is *her* voice under Jenny's plaintive "I didn't mean anything in the world!" It is *Glasgow*'s awakening that gives this novel, and all her mature novels, their authenticity, their authority, their bitter power. In *The Woman Within* she wrote sadly, "It had taken me sixty years to discover that there was nothing to be done either about my own life or about the world in which I lived"[17]—except to draw it so clearly that readers could not forget it; to, in fact, etch it with her own stringently denunciatory words.

CHAPTER 7

Vein of Iron

Published in 1935 when Glasgow was sixty-two, her eighteenth novel is in some ways her richest. Many central themes from *Barren Ground* and the novels of manners reappear—those of individual determination in conflict with social pressure, of the importance of establishing a personal belief, of endurance and generosity, of family traditions and loyalties, of romantic love and love beyond that, and of the artistic (and/or feminine) struggle for fruition—and are effectively melded into the principal narratives of John Fincastle and his daughter Ada. That the novel encompasses thirty years rather than a few months makes clear Glasgow's emphasis on development, on the evolution of character, as her title also suggests. After she had found that readers sometimes misread the title *Barren Ground* (and viewed Dorinda Oakley as defeated instead of productive), Glasgow this time chose to be directive in her title: characters with the vein of iron were survivors. Throughout her work Glasgow had used the phrase to describe some of her favorite achieving characters. The novel's working title had been *The Will to Live* (*L.*, 163).

Working with this longer time span, Glasgow also had the opportunity to create an entire world, this one the Scots-Presbyterian village of Ironside in Virginia's Shut-in Valley. The map which serves as frontispiece for the novel shows the clear mental image she carried of the fictional area. Curious as Glasgow had been about the Scotch beliefs and character as they were evidenced in her own family, she allowed herself time—both at the beginning of the novel and at important intervals throughout—to explore these traditions. That these segments of the book were personally important to her seems clear from her notes:

> These first settlers, called Scotch-Irish, were religious pioneers, and in some cases brought over their Presbyterian congregations. . . .
> The truth is, of course, that the Scottish mind is incurably metaphysical. The doctrine of predestination, for example, is an excursion into pure metaphysics.[1]

In *Vein of Iron* Glasgow succeeds in merging scene and character so that both are effective: the scene, in fact, seems to have directly influenced the characters' development. Glasgow gives much attention early in the novel to the ancestry of the Fincastle family; the strong currents of fortitude and morality—so intrepid as to seem maverick—that surged through individual family members were enhanced by the isolation of the Virginia village. In Ironside the Fincastles could maintain their sense of purpose, their direction. Once they moved to Queenborough, however, the sheer weight of other attitudes began to undermine their beliefs, and in some cases, centers of purpose were shaken. This plot development is prompted by Glasgow's curiosity, expressed in her 1938 preface to the novel, about "the resolute breed from which my father had sprung":

> Having held fast through the generations, would this breed yield nowadays to the disintegrating forces in the modern world? Would that instinct for survival we used to call "the soul of man" be content to wear, for the future, the tarnished label of "psychology"? Would those intrepid Scottish metaphysicians, who had placed freedom to believe above freedom to doubt, and had valued immaterial safety more than material comfort, would they sink, in the end, under the dead weight of an age that believed only in the machine? (*CM*, 168)

Glasgow's constant sense of involvement with her characters—shown in this novel through her use of internal monologue rather than omniscient point of view—also allows the reader to feel empathy with most of the characters in *Vein of Iron*.

The novel is the story, primarily, of John Fincastle, outcast minister turned outcast philosopher, and his daughter Ada, whose search for romance provides the plot for the first half of the novel. Fincastle himself represents the wide learning, the passionate love of knowledge, that had marked Glasgow's own life. As she explained in her notes, "For twenty years, in my early youth, my chief interest was the study of philosophy; and all that I read and thought was embodied in my favorite character [John Fincastle]."[2] A social outcast because of his agnosticism, Fincastle is known among European philosophers for his four-volume work *God as Idea*. Poverty keeps him teaching school in Ironside, and then in Queenborough, however, where he faces his life of ridicule and deprivation with equanimity. He is the isolate, the misunderstood, the otherworldly, the artist-scholar who survives despite an unaccepting culture. As years pass, he also becomes the personification of altruism. He assumes the qualities of his strong mother, loving the most common people of his community and moving, eventually, far from his philosophical studies. When the famous German scholar comes to visit at the close of Fincastle's life, he wonders bemusedly what language this is that philosophers try to share; he finds that he can better understand the simple Midkiff, with whom he stands in bread lines. Much of Fincastle's character springs from Glasgow's own, of course, if it is viewed as the prototype not of American man so much as that of American writer.

Ada Fincastle is the continuation of Glasgow's willful female persona. Although she loves her family deeply, she is never bound by their ideas of suitable behavior, especially Christian behavior. We see her at age seven, compassionate for the retarded child who is being abused by the other village children. Of them, only Ada sees the pathos in the boy's mistreatment; she gives him her cap to replace his own filthy one. Like her father, she too is an outsider, showing kindness for animals and people, questioning moral codes. Ada is motivated primarily by her own sense of need, and one of those needs throughout the novel is the love of Ralph McBride, whose child she bears even after he has married Janet Rowan. Another need is that of fidelity to the cause of family— her grandmother, Aunt Meggie, her mother and father. It is a cruel irony that her pregnancy out of wedlock pushes her grandmother close to death. Ada, not comprehending the strength of the woman's moral position, has inadvertently grieved the aging woman past recovery. She rouses once, to help deliver Ada's child, but she soon dies, leaving a great sense of loss within the family.

Glasgow uses the character of Ada in somewhat the same way she did that of Dorinda Oakley, to show what a woman's life can become after she has lived past the tragedy of sexual betrayal. Whereas Dorinda lost her child and was able to live as if she had never known love or passion, Ada was forced to live with the evidence of that involvement. The battles spring from the same source; Ada has a relatively complex series of decisions to make throughout her life with Ralph. When Glasgow fuses the images—Ada's seeing herself chased by children both as a child and as an unmarried mother—she reminds her readers that decisions obscure artificial divisions in time. Ada's choices shape her life regardless of years. Janet's tongue being painted with quinine because she lied remains an apt image for her, just as Ada's being punished for unnamed faults, unconscious faults, remains her pervasive image.

In dividing her sympathies within *Vein of Iron* so that both John Fincastle and Ada can be called protagonists, Glasgow halted a tendency developing during her novels of manners. More often than not, the very women who would have been mere ornaments in Glasgow's early fiction (because they were unaware, unquestioning, chained to tradition) have become heroines. Victoria Littlepage in *They Stooped to Folly* is certainly reminiscent of Lucy Pendleton, yet in this novel she eclipses the stronger woman, Louisa Goddard. Eva Birdsong in *The Sheltered Life* has had precisely the education and motivation of Virginia Pendleton; while she is not a heroine per se, she is one center of the tragic focus.

What Glasgow had evidently come to realize, once she had grown past the somewhat romantic tendency of thinking that a person had only to declare independence in order to become independent, was that most women were caught in irrevocable social and economic circumstances, and that most of them chose to lead their lives within those confines. In real life, not every thoughtful woman was a rebel. In order to draw recognizable women, she needed to focus on those seemingly conventional people who yet managed to live nobly. Such characters were not, finally, prototypes for the kind of women Glasgow herself preferred, women like Dorinda Oakley. By the time of *Vein of Iron*, it seems that Glasgow is resigned to divide her persona: the isolated philosopher-artist is pictured as male; the person searching for love is female. Because each character shares traits of the author's, one might suggest that Glasgow was relinquishing the attempt at self-portraiture she had anticipated so well in *Barren Ground*. She was also creating characters that readers would be more likely to accept as realistic.

The double protagonists of *Vein of Iron* also suggest that Glasgow saw her own role in life, as woman and as writer, as paradoxical. In the matter of romance, for example, we have seen throughout her fiction the struggle to find a satisfying romantic relationship. Most of her female characters spend their energy and time in this pursuit, even those who do not find a devoted gentleman waiting at the end of their lives. In Ada Fincastle, Glasgow portrays a passionate woman who loves with "single heart"; but in the character of John Fincastle, all such concepts are strangely distanced. One of the most interesting passages in the novel shows Fincastle thinking of the deep love he has shared with his beautiful wife, Mary Evelyn, yet realizing that that human part of his life is in some ways unimportant. His expression of the conflict between needing love and needing solitude for his work speaks to Glasgow's conflicts as well:

> Deep within his consciousness, so deep that the wish had never floated to the surface of thought, there was a buried regret for the solitary ways of the heart. . . . all the outward aspects of living seemed to him fragmentary, unreal, and fugitive. He had not willed

this; he had struggled against the sense of exile that divided him from the thought of his time, from his dearest, his nearest. Nevertheless, it was there. His inner life alone, the secret life of the soul, was vital and intimate and secure.[3]

The inherent loneliness for this person's beloved is a given for the relationship, as Fincastle goes on to recognize: "Well, he had loved her. No woman, only his seeking mind, had ever divided them. He would have given all he was for her, but he could not give what he was not; he could not make himself over; he could not prevent that involuntary recoil now and then, as if his whole existence were overgrown and smothered by the natures of women. Even the wincing of his nerves while her voice ran on, strained, bright, monotonous, inexpressibly sweet, was beyond his control" (50). Again, in his death scene, Fincastle cannot remember his wife's name: he is a child, he cares only for his mother. Such candor had seldom ever appeared in Glasgow's work, whether she was speaking of herself or of a character; and in this case, surely she was speaking of both. That Fincastle was her favorite character stems partly from the fact that through him she was able to express the sometimes contradictory feelings she had known in her own eventful life as woman—and as that most complex of persons, woman writer.

Subtly, Glasgow emphasizes the otherworldliness of John Fincastle's passion by contrasting it with the primary love story of the novel. It is Ada's love for Ralph McBride that dominates her life, and Glasgow uses the tenacity and passion of Ada's love to illustrate her personal vein of iron. Yet all the difficulties in that relationship occur, not because of any fault of Ada's—despite her repeated pronouncements of guilt—but because Ralph cannot be faithful. His flirtation with Janet that leads to his marriage, with the German women during the war, and finally with the sixteen-year-old Minna are documented clearly if ironically. Ada blames herself at every turn for her "pride," "anger," "jealousy": her family reacts with the disappointed if silent acceptance of the double standard (men—most men—are like this). Ralph takes refuge in his customary diffidence, withholding from Ada any word of either apology or love. That she accepts him, despite his implicit contrast to her father—whose love for his wife remains single, despite his intellectual remoteness—must be disappointing to the modern reader. The fault of "the single heart" which her grandmother lamented early in the novel remained Ada's. She loved unreservedly and, in the eyes of this reader, undeservedly.

As if to emphasize the foolishness of Ada's passion for Ralph, Glasgow creates almost melodramatic consequences for her actions. Once Ralph marries Janet, Ada waits for his return. Not only has she been heartbroken in the jilting, she waits—patiently—for six years on the basis of a spidery suggestion from Ralph that sometime Janet will want a divorce. Not only does Ada wait: she also lies to her family in order to make love with Ralph, and in so doing, becomes pregnant.

The pattern is established: for Ralph's whim, Ada and Ada's family pay. After the accident in Queenborough, Ralph's long hospitalization and mysterious paralysis wipe out nearly all the family savings (the Depression accomplishes the rest). Ralph is also left even more embittered, becoming both a psychological and physical burden. Because Ada had cajoled him (on the very day of his meeting with Minna and the accident) about their having another child, Glasgow's use of this plot device also suggests Ralph's desire to avoid any more responsibility, any fuller involvement with Ada. To list the events of Ada's life as results of Ralph's flirtations would be to list betrayal, six years of abandonment, scandal, separation from family, an illegitimate child, change of home, severe poverty and want—for both Ada and her family. Even John Fincastle's death from intentional starvation can be attributed to the poverty that resulted from Ralph's last folly. The tranquil tone of the narrative belies the intensity of Glasgow's condemnation.

One must, at some point, connect the character of Ralph McBride—impractical, volatile, "Irish"—with the men in Glasgow's own life. Whether they physically resemble Ralph is less important than the fact that they consistently disappoint Ada/Glasgow. After the great passion of their illicit mountain tryst, Ralph's letters to Ada are stolid, noncommittal, stingy. After their marriage, Ralph's moments of tenderness are rare. The novel, in fact, focuses on those moments as though they were great crescendos of emotion—only to drop Ada down after each instance into an inexpressible sense of loss: Ralph's words about wanting a daughter precede his ultimate betrayal with a teenager. The ending dialogue, following John Fincastle's magnificent struggle to die in Ironside, is again so chary and bland that the reader wonders at Ada's being able to accept it. Contrasted with the devotion her father had shown his wife, the fragile Mary Evelyn, Ralph's inarticulate and emotionless commitment to Ada seems to express the defeated modern spirit.

Perhaps that was one of Glasgow's wider ironies, the great difference in the expectations of generations. The earlier Fincastles prayed only for survival; they lived among warring Indians, deprivations, bereavements. "Time and again, they had risen from the ruins of happiness. Yet they had gone on; they had rebuilt the ruins, they had scattered life more abundantly over the ashes. . . . they also had loved life. They had loved it the more . . . because it was fugitive" (40). Ada received that inheritance, as her grandmother would admonish her,

> Remember, my child, that you have strong blood. . . . Never let
> it be weakened. Thin blood runs to wickedness. (21)

Ralph McBride, on the other hand, had expected success (first as a lawyer, then as a car salesman); passion (if not with Ada or Janet, then with various partners); gratitude (just for being himself, as his mother consistently reinforced). That he did little to achieve success in either business or love never occurred to him. For all his natural talent, Ralph lacked the essential integrity the Fincastle family built upon: the vein of iron. It was easier for him not to fight social pressure and marry Janet, easier not to return from war, easier not to get out of the hospital— Ralph's motivation was that of ease, whereas John Fincastle's seemed to be that of pain.

Glasgow's commentary on the younger generation, the emphasis on the *I* and on the quest for personal pleasure, dominates the last third of *Vein of Iron*. Both Ada and her father react against the shallow lives that surround them—Fincastle as he teaches teenage girls with painted faces in a private school, Ada as she sells gloves in a department store ("They're different, these women, and they're all alike, she thought. . . . 'I, I, I, I . . .' Never an end. Always the bright, blank current, eager, empty, grasping, insatiable . . ." 277). Ralph never shares in their censure; he in fact adopts much of the behavior, as his flirtation with the young Minna is intended to show.

As Glasgow/Ada saw it, the real problems of the modern Queenborough generation were twofold: the pressure to conform and the tendency to "disremember the past," to live "without a foundation." Glasgow presents Ada's recognition of these problems didactically, because she believes in their importance:

> In Ironside, poor as they were, they had built upon rock. Now in
> Queenborough, it seemed to her, life was an air plant, springing up
> out of emptiness. Vapor it was yesterday, and vapor it would be
> again tomorrow. All that she had thought of as enduring forever had
> apparently melted away. (277)

The novel, accordingly, turns on Ada's anxiety to get the family back to Ironside, to the beloved if decrepit manse. That direction, however, is complicated by the ever-deepening poverty the Fincastles experience. Finally, only a few days from eviction and Aunt Meg's being sent to the poorhouse, the McBride-Fincastle family is saved by the grotesque but heroic journey of John Fincastle to Ironside for his own death and burial. Once he dies there near the manse, and the family does return, they decide to stay. Here they recover their sense of family and purpose. The ending scenes are short, but Glasgow makes use of her leisurely beginning, particularly of the grandmother's impression of the manse when she had first arrived as a bride:

> Everything had seemed to her to be provided; the grove of oaks to cast shade; the vegetable garden at the back of the house; the well so close to the kitchen porch; the springhouse at the bottom of the yard under the big willow; and the house inside, with the solid furniture, the rows of books that had always been there, and the shining pewter plates, so bright you could see your face in them. (38–39)

What was most impressive was its sense of history: "All the generations which had been a part. . . . The solid roof overhead, the solid floor underfoot, the fears of the night without, the flames and the shadows of flames within . . . were all mingled now" (46). The role of the manse in *Vein of Iron* parallels that of the land in *Barren Ground*, and so Ada returns to her source as Dorinda had returned to hers. But in *Vein of Iron* there is less of the sense of conflict. Ada returns to a more supportive place, filled with memories of loving, strong people. There is communication here, and respect for people's talents, and insight far beyond the mere observance of social convention. Rhetoric has no place in the Fincastle vocabulary, and the health with which the characters speak and relate is new to Glasgow's pictures of the Virginia Tidewater society: "Words are only stale air" (137). In *Barren Ground*, only Dorinda could sense the discrepancy between what characters said and their intent; and understanding in her case became an irony rather than a comfort.

Glasgow recalls in her preface to the later novel that the two books have much in common: "I was reviving the substance and the manner of *Barren Ground*";[4] and further: "I was trying to isolate, not a single character or group of characters alone, but the vital principle of survival."[5] She refers to *fortitude* again, and the autobiographical implications of a woman character who finds no fulfillment in marriage—or, indeed, never comes to marriage—and whose physical circumstances have done nothing but impair her progress (as Glasgow felt about her early deafness) are obvious. "Ada was nearest me in many ways," Glasgow says with candor, and that identification helps create the emotional reality of many of Ada's scenes. Glasgow gives us reality of the spirit, that detailed, loving sense of happiness, or bereavement, or dismay, or disbelief.

As Glasgow said firmly in her 1934 *Saturday Review* essay, "One Way to Write Novels," "A novelist must write, not by taking thought alone, but with every cell of his being, that nothing can occur to him that may not sooner or later find its way into his craft. . . . Because everything one has seen or heard or thought or felt leaves a deposit that never filters entirely through the essence of mind, I believe a novelist should be perpetually engaged in this effort to refresh and replenish his source. I am confident, moreover, that nothing I have learned either from life or from literature has been wasted."[6] In a 1935 letter, she speaks more directly about the genesis of *Vein of Iron*,

> The book did not require notes. . . . *Vein of Iron* was torn up by the roots from the experience and observation and reflection of a lifetime. . . . The novel had always existed below the surface of thought; and for the three years while I was actually writing it, I lived in a state of total immersion.[7]

Vein of Iron, then, like *Barren Ground* and *Virginia*, seems to have been another of those novels whose writing was a culmination, a bringing to fruition artistically of the joys and traumas of personal as well as literary existence. Riding on the success of *The Sheltered Life*, Glasgow must have felt herself ready to attempt what she saw from the start as a continuation of *Barren Ground*, the book that had exhausted her because of its proximity to her personal life and tragedy. Here, Ada was to parallel Dorinda, and each character's resemblance to Glasgow is clear. Having turned sixty, Glasgow also had to know that *Vein of Iron* might well be her last novel (see *L.*, 194). To face the three-year process of forcing memory and knowledge into writing was a task that, however challenging, could also be psychologically dangerous ("torn up by the roots"). Perhaps Glasgow's using John Fincastle to express the artist/philosopher was one way of protecting herself from more personal revelations than she was capable of making at that time. A few years later, however, as she wrote the candid autobiography *The Woman Within*, she was able to write about herself as artist and to say many of the same things about Ellen Glasgow that she had earlier written about Fincastle. As she wrote in 1935, "With John Fincastle, I treat of the fate, the isolation, of the scholar in America, of the thinker among the dynamos" (*L.*, 191). The sense of exile as well as isolation was clear in both their lives.

When Glasgow describes the themes of *Vein of Iron* to John Chamberlain, also in 1935, she makes plain that the novel is the story of a family rather than of a single character, and of that family's success as a family unit. In most of Glasgow's fiction, characters succeed at least partly because they break with family attitudes, particularly during formative years. The tragedy of many lives which Glasgow describes is that they fear the break and continue in patterns and beliefs that hold no meaning for them. She clarifies to Chamberlain that, even though Ada and Ralph eventually return to Ironside, the novel is in no way "a defense of the old order." It is meant to be, rather, a study of endurance:

> What I tried to do was to look through human nature and human behavior, and discover the motives, or qualities of endurance, that have enabled mankind to survive in any order under the sun. Through each individual in a family group, I have tried to trace this hidden motive, this vein of iron, which had held the generations together. Religion. Philosophy. Young love. Simple human relationships. Or the unbreakable will to live that we call fortitude.[8]

As she says in her notes for *Vein of Iron*, "Fortitude is the ultimate virtue."[9]

Glasgow's emphasis on basic human beliefs, expressed through close personal ties, might seem foreign to her early years devoted to philosophy. After years of seeming to force characters into philosophical stances that she found viable, she appears to have relaxed into knowledge which could come as readily from human experience as from study. As J. R. Raper points out, Glasgow's final vision is one of possibility, a view tempered with a mixture of realism and idealism and not based entirely on intellectual response.[10] It is to that mediating posture that Fincastle himself returns late in life.

Technically, Glasgow structures *Vein of Iron* to emphasize the novel's concern with the Fincastle family, particularly those family members of whom she speaks in her letter to Chamberlain. One important early sec-

tion of *Vein of Iron*—chapters four through eight—is given to a series of
five monologues, each spoken by one person in the intimate family:
Grandmother Fincastle, Aunt Meg, Ada, John, and Mary Evelyn. In
this novel the Fincastle family remains central; all other characters—
even Ralph McBride and Ranny—are peripheral.

For Glasgow to turn to interior monologue even in part, after years of
her careful omniscient perspective, is both to repeat the success she had
known in some sections of *Barren Ground* and *They Stooped to Folly* and
also to break with what had become her convention in the trilogy of
manners. Just as detached perspective was not the appropriate vehicle
for *Vein of Iron*, neither was irony:

> Sophisticated wit and sparkling irony must be drained away from
> this bare and steady chronicle of simple lives. And so the speech of
> the heart, not the language of the mind, must serve as the revealing
> medium for my narrative. . . . Satire would have splintered back
> from the sober bulk of the Presbyterian mind and conscience. A
> natural vehicle, the grave speech of a spiritually proud and materi-
> ally humble race . . . was the one inevitable expression for my
> novel.[11]

Even though Glasgow also felt that the story must be told from the perspectives of both Ada and John Fincastle, her introduction of the other
major characters was more forceful since it was accomplished through
this "speech of the heart." Once she had decided to write the five "re-
flective views" of the family members, she found that "it took me
months to enter completely into the mental processes of these five different human beings . . . to immerse myself in their separate moods
and visions."[12]

One of the most difficult ways to characterize speakers was through
rhythm. Glasgow describes the pace of the grandmother's section as
"slow, rocking," while Mary Evelyn's section moved through "flashes
of insight," and Ada's "in staccato cadences."[13] What Glasgow was cap-
turing entire, of course, was the full ambience of characterization—the
movement, the typical imagery, the kinds of attitude and content pecu-
liar to all the best-drawn characters in her fictional world. She acknowledged that "after I had written these chapters, I felt that there was little
left for me to learn about the inner lives of my characters."[14]

What the reader remembers from grandmother's monologue is her
physical endurance: "'Twas the three cups of coffee that put the heart
into me and will make me sleep sound"; "Bending over with difficulty,

she eased her foot, which had begun to swell"; "She had enjoyed every-thing, even childbirth." The deaths of her husband and seven of their children, poverty, her son John's trial for heresy—these sorrows had only tempered her. Glasgow slows the tempo of her vigor by casting her in a twilight mood; her health is more fragile than she knows:

> A closed memory unfolded as a fan in her thoughts. She saw the
> pale red loop of the road round the manse on a spring morning, the
> narrow valley, deep as a river, and the Endless Mountains thronging
> under the April blue of the sky. More than fifty years ago, but it
> seemed only yesterday! From the changeless past and the slow ac-
> cretion of time, the day and the scene emerged into the firelight . . .
> from the falling leaves . . . and the sifting dust . . . and the cob-
> webs . . . and the mildew.[15]

Of that section, Glasgow writes in the novel's preface, "Grandmother's retrospect moves with a slow, rocking vibration, as when one is reluc-tantly falling asleep, and grows fainter and farther away as drowsiness conquers" (xvii). The chapter, however, ends focused outward to Ada and her father, and with that focus Glasgow's pace quickens.

The balanced sentences and incremental structures continue from Grandmother's section into John's; the sonority is broken throughout both by questions, usually in series, and by emphatic sentences. John Fincastle's pace is restless. Often he begins with a well-phrased gener-ality which would be easily supported:

> No man who has to provide for a family, John Fincastle thought,
> has a right to search after truth. (48)

Glasgow then immediately undercuts that assurance: "Perhaps not any-where in the world. Certainly not in America. . . . He didn't know. He couldn't pretend to care."

Fincastle's narrative is poignant in his attempts to understand his own direction. He mulls over his life and education in balanced sen-tences, yet these are frequently interrupted by disruptive phrases: "His world, he knew, was not, and could never become, the world of facts; he was, and would always remain, out of touch with what men call real-ities" (49).

Like his mother, John too recalls the strong women of the family, particularly his grandmother Margaret Graham. He knows her for her courage in rearing her children alone, for her learning, for her "invincible poise." His mother knew her as the bearer of the aristocratic Scotch lineage (the Montrose), and through the fusion of those memories Glasgow takes us back to the theme of inherited strengths. John Fincastle may not have firm intellectual answers at this point in his life, but if he continues to trust to his own recognition, he will find ways to "reconcile" the will and the intellect.

The breathlessness of Mary Evelyn's monologue ("I've forgotten something . . . but I can't think what it is") leads to Glasgow's summary, "Flightiness was her infirmity"; but by the time we reach chapter six, we already know the physical reasons for her being distraught. Ill health, hypertensive nerves, a magnanimity few human beings could support—Mary Evelyn is the image of self-abnegation. Her section begins and ends with her concern for Ada; the child must be happy. Her thoughts, in their short rapidly ranging sentences, turn consistently to her family, "the glowing center of life" (55). "She had much to be thankful for. Nobody was ill; nobody was hungry; nobody she loved was out in the cold. Aunt Abigail had a good fire, and Horace . . . was warm on the hearth" (56). What Glasgow achieves in her creation of Mary Evelyn's distraction is the sense of a person pushed beyond coherence, a person who seeks the center in a thousand small physical details rather than through large overriding principles. Given the circumstances of the Fincastle family, particularly their poverty, Mary Evelyn's battle to order the details of their life is doomed to failure.

Aunt Meggie's stolidity in chapter seven is not without its warmth. Her personal loneliness disappears in her role within the family; her firm Christian beliefs give her a tranquility that seems unshakable. Meggie faces poverty, mice, and outing flannel nightgowns with equanimity; only spiders threaten her. As Glasgow summarized, "She had put her hope in little things, and she had been happy. She was the only member of the family who was never low-spirited, not even in the long winters" (60).

Ada's closing monologue moves like her mother's as it ranges from the taste of sugar to her new doll to a Christmas adventure with Ralph to spiders to household chores. One long passage deals with Ada's sympathy for animals out in the cold, and another with the necessity for idiots like Toby Waters; the monologue culminates in her finally accepting the china-haired doll by taking it to bed with her.

The monologue leaves us with Ada's tendency to create, to enjoy her imagination ("The taste of sugar is like pinks . . . verbena and sweet alyssum," 61). She impresses with her capacity to feel, and we try to discount the similarities Glasgow points to between Mary Evelyn and her child.

These five monologues close book one of *Vein of Iron*. Book two opens with Ada, now twenty, engaged to Ralph, and we once more revisit the *Barren Ground* story of betrayal and anguish. Throughout this narrative, however, Ada is surrounded by her family. What Glasgow gains by playing the Ada-Ralph romance against that of her parents is important: we see the ideal; we see why Ada expects her love with Ralph to be fulfilling. In *Barren Ground*, Dorinda was building largely on fantasy; she was trying to find a unique experience. Ada wants only what she has already witnessed, a love that lasts to death. When her mother dies and Ralph—now married to Janet—comes to pay his respects, Ada is able to express the great love she had for her mother, and with that tribute the key to Mary Evelyn's life:

Nothing makes any difference but the thought that Mother . . . oh, Mother . . .
She would want you to be happy.
She believed in happiness. Feeling meant life to her. It is only in the heart, she used to say, that anything really happens. (181)

The union between John Fincastle and Ada after Mary Evelyn's death helps to clarify the similarities Glasgow had been describing in their attitudes toward possessions, people, and purpose in life. Neither had ever wanted material wealth. John Fincastle's disdain for comfort was legendary. Working long hours without a fire in his study, his head covered with one of his wife's scarfs, he forgets food in his need to create. Ada too longs only for a few objects with personal value; her reverence for Mary Evelyn's blue bowl was more a tribute to her mother's ability to create beauty than it was a need to possess.

By the end of the novel, Fincastle and Ada are very much alike in their realization of the importance of the human spirit: all people must be valued. One of the reasons they can relate so easily to people, Glasgow emphasizes, is that they themselves can understand fear. Never judgmental as was Grandmother Fincastle, both John and Ada sense themselves outside the elect. Just as Ada has nightmares of being chased by cruel children, so Fincastle himself, nearing death, is privy to the same kind of fear. He finds himself surrounded by a jeering family of idiots—"A world of idiots . . . To escape from them, to run away, he must break through not only a throng, but a whole world" (456). Sweating so that "every pore seemed dripping with fear," Fincastle manages to go on, out of his dream, so that he can literally die at home; and there, with Ada, he realizes the wisdom of the simple refrain,

May all that have life be delivered from suffering. (448)

The ending of *Vein of Iron*, then, acts as the whole novel has, to move far beyond the relatively single endings of *Barren Ground*, the trilogy novels, and *The Battle-Ground*—endings in which a primary plot line does conclude. *Vein of Iron* is truly a novel about the way all human beings must live. When Glasgow had directed herself, in her notes for the novel, to make the figure of John Fincastle "bigger and broader in sweep" and to add in part two "many more characters" so that the "range widens," she saw clearly where *Vein of Iron* was ultimately to end. She describes that too:

As sense of individual responsibility becomes weaker, communal (civil) responsibility necessarily increases.[16]

For John Fincastle to move beyond his own ego-centered search for truth so that he might give life to his family and friends—whether it be through his insurance money or through friendship in the bread line— was the same kind of self-abnegation that Ada faced when she had to choose between renouncing Ralph for his unfaithfulness or keeping her family intact. For all its trappings of romantic novel, *Vein of Iron* is never that: Ada is pictured more often as the daughter of the Fincastles than the wife of a McBride.

The latter condition, in fact, seems almost temporary, and the concluding scene is perhaps best understood as an illustration of that impermanence. If *Vein of Iron* were primarily a romantic novel, the closing dialogue between Ada and Ralph would be most disappointing. Here once again the lovers are starting over, but what a change from the very similar ending of *The Battle-Ground* (when Betty Ambler says to Dan, "We will begin again . . . and this time, my dear, we will begin together").[17] Here Ada and Ralph exist not as lovers but rather as friends who have learned to exist despite broken illusions. Glasgow cannot resist giving Ada the greater courage, as Ralph acknowledges ("You're a dreamer, Ada. It's queer that a dreamer should be a rock to lean on"), but the thrust of the ending is that Ralph and Ada are in themselves only links: their role is to keep the family alive. Rather than the final scene between Ada and Ralph, this passage may be the true ending of the novel:

> "Are you sure, then, that we're coming back? I was only half serious."
> "Yes. I'm sure. I felt it from the beginning." She had a sense, more a feeling than a vision, of the dead generations behind her. They had come to life there in the past; they were lending her their fortitude; they were reaching out to her in adversity. This was the heritage they had left. She could lean back on their strength; she could recover that lost certainty of a continuing tradition.
> "It will be starting over from the very bottom."
> "Well, we're at the bottom, so it's high time for us to start."
> "Have you thought of Ranny?"
> "I've thought of him every minute." (461)

The Fincastle line would go on, even in the McBride, and Glasgow's intense novel had presented imagistically the substance of her own late philosophical statement:

> Because the church has evaded these issues and imprisoned its faith in arbitrary doctrines, I think it has failed to satisfy the intellectual and spiritual needs of the modern world, in which primitive consecrations and barbaric symbols have lost, for many of us, their earlier significance. Yet I think, too, that the mass of men will not be content to live entirely without religion or philosophy as a guide.
> And, finally, beyond this, I can see only the vanishing-point in the perspective, where all beliefs disappear and the deepest certainties, if they exist, cannot be comprehended by the inquiring mind alone, but must be apprehended by that inmost reason which we may call the heart.[18]

"It is only in the heart that anything really happens."

CHAPTER 8

The Last Years

Partly because *Vein of Iron* served as the culmination of many themes throughout Glasgow's earlier fiction, she was well satisfied with the book ("I think it is all beautiful and wonderful"; "my best and biggest and truest novel"; "it had been simmering in my mind for many years").[1] Had it been, in fact, her last book, *Vein of Iron* would have been a fitting conclusion. Because Glasgow wrote for nearly another decade, the fact that her work after this novel does little more than extend these themes is not surprising. It may be that much of Glasgow's attention during the last decade of her life went to her critical prefaces, in which she could express her views of both fiction and life, and to her autobiography, *The Woman Within*, which did much the same.

Between 1935, when *Vein of Iron* was published, and 1945, when Glasgow died in her sleep after a six-year heart condition, she wrote and published the prefaces to the twelve novels included in Scribner's Virginia Edition. These important essays, and the preface she wrote for her 1941 *In This Our Life*, were collected and published in 1943 as *A Certain Measure*. Glasgow's writings about theory gave her great pride; she felt that their publication greatly enhanced her reputation as a writer.[2]

In 1937 she had also begun *In This Our Life*, the novel which was to be published in 1941, but these were years of increasingly poor health for Glasgow, and progress on this novel was frequently interrupted. The project that seems to have interested her more, to which she refers as early as 1935, was her autobiography. Given the reticence of much of her fiction, given the fact that she chose male characters to image the artist, Glasgow's willingness to attempt autobiography indicated some change in her self-image. Indeed, as Patricia Meyer Spacks has observed,

> Relatively few women have asserted themselves unambiguously as shaping artists in the act of writing about themselves; even Anais Nin, whose self-glorification as artist and as woman parallels Isadora Duncan's, publishes diaries rather than formal autobiography.[3]

The Woman Within was published posthumously (1954) as Glasgow had directed, by Irita Van Doren and Frank V. Morley, her literary executors. The extreme care Glasgow took with the preservation of the manuscript after the book's completion is evidence of its great personal value.[4]

Glasgow experienced severe heart attacks both in 1939 and 1940, but she managed to write, if only for fifteen minutes a day, during her long periods of convalescence. When *In This Our Life* was finally completed and published, to good if inaccurate reviews, she felt it a personal triumph. Sold to Hollywood, the novel became a popular movie starring Bette Davis, Olivia de Haviland, and Dennis Morgan. The novel also won for Glasgow her first Pulitzer Prize (in 1940 she had been honored with the prestigious Howells Medal from the American Academy of Arts and Letters). Dissatisfied with the nihilistic reading many critics had given *In This Our Life*, she felt compelled to write a sequel, the very short manuscript which was completed in 1944. She finally chose not to publish *Beyond Defeat*, but it was published by Luther Y. Gore in 1966.

Hardly the embarrassment some critics claim them to be, Glasgow's last novels—*In This Our Life* and *Beyond Defeat*—offer some interesting variations to Glasgow's other fiction. Written to expose the frightening absence of "family feeling" in modern life (this phrase is the title of part one), *In This Our Life* presents strong characters as well as weak. Asa Timberlake, the fifty-nine-year-old factory worker who has supported his family uncomplainingly up to this time, and his perspicacious older daughter, Roy, are wholly admirable. They withstand sorrow and injustice without becoming bitter. The Timberlake family is itself the stuff of soap opera—a pouting sexpot of a younger sister, a rich uncle and dowager aunt, a suicidal son-in-law, an invalid mother, cheerful if deprived blacks—and in that respect the novel founders, but the weak characters are balanced by the stability of Asa and Roy. That they are martyrs for the family is one of Glasgow's points, but even though some members of the family fail to appreciate them, they care for themselves and for each other. As Glasgow insisted when Warner Brothers was planning the film,

> If only they will emphasize the father and daughter theme, and bring out the character of Asa. . . . I suppose it is futile to suggest that the movie shall make a kind of "Mr. Chips" picture, treating Asa Timberlake as the major figure, instead of playing up the subject of callow youth or broken marriages? (*L.*, 281, 280)

That the film did not do this was, of course, further reason for Glasgow's anger.[5]

Aside from the father-daughter theme, *In This Our Life* portrays with a vengeance the coddled Lavinia whose ill health has tyrannized her family, especially her self-sacrificing husband Asa; and the irresponsible younger sister Stanley, who not only steals her sister's husband but kills a child in a hit-and-run accident. There is no question about either Stanley's depravity or the favoritism shown her by the family, no matter what she does. The immorality of much of the family stems from the mother's warped judgment, and the partial treatment of Stanley only illustrates these values.

The older sister, Roy, is reasonably strong, but she has always been the outsider. Loved by her ineffectual father, she has learned to respond to true affection, but she is helpless to play games for power. Her marriage to Peter cannot withstand Stanley's machinations: here again Glasgow uses the theme of betrayal, but this time the woman is jilted not by a lover but by a husband, left not for a stranger but for her own sister. Incest of a sort darkens Glasgow's image of the modern age.

Aside from this darkening of tone, however, many themes of *In This Our Life* are similar to those of Glasgow's early fiction. Place and the sense of belonging are crucial: the novel opens with Asa's mourning the destruction of an old home which is being torn down to make way for a gas station. Asa and his family live in a new but shoddy home. They have no sense of permanence and, in fact, the members of the Timberlake family speed past each other in cars of every description. There is little family life as such. Asa laments the family's loss of position: his grandfather had once owned the factory in which he works. More than financial position, however, Asa mourns lost values: convenience, speed, and pleasure have replaced integrity and virtue. Even the fact that his grandfather—faced with incurable illness—committed suicide under the old willow is a positive image when set against the mean invalidism of Asa's wife.

Asa's sorrow is obviously an extension of that of John and Ada Fincastle in *Vein of Iron*, but all of *In This Our Life* takes place in the present (1938). Whereas the Fincastles could remember better times and hope to return to them, Asa can escape from the present only by spending Sundays with his friend Kate Oliver and her dogs. On Kate's farm, close to the calm center of both earth and friendship, Asa is happy. His yearning to leave Lavinia, epitome of modern selfishness, is his motivation throughout the novel. That he supports his family through one catastrophe after another, that he remains with Lavinia even at the close of the novel, led some readers to see him as defeated. That view was

clearly not Glasgow's intention. She had used bird imagery throughout
the novel to suggest incipient freedom, and she closes the book with
Asa's tranquil acceptance of yet another delay in his path to freedom—
but the sense of that freedom brings the novel to its end.

> Looking up at the closed sky, once again he had a vision of Kate
> and the harvested fields and the broad river. Still ahead, and within
> sight, but just out of reach, and always a little farther away, fading,
> but not ever disappearing, was freedom.[6]

Asa could still dream; he was in no way unfulfilled. "We have our-
selves," he is to insist at the end of *Beyond Defeat*.[7]

Glasgow felt that the sequel novel, with its explicit title, was necessary to show readers that Asa could find happiness. In the three years
that passed between books, Asa has gone to live and work on the Oliver
farm (pressed into service by World War II and its demands for productive farms). He has found happiness even though Lavinia thinks that
his act has disgraced her. By the time of *Beyond Defeat*, however,
Glasgow seems less interested in Asa's personal happiness and more
concerned with showing that he has gotten back to roots, sources, stability. Perhaps most important, he has escaped the malaise of modern
life. As Glasgow wrote in 1942,

> The problem I had set myself was an analysis in fiction of the
> modern temper; and the modern temper, as it pressed round me, in
> a single community, appeared confused, vacillating, uncertain, and
> distracted from permanent values. . . . Asa Timberlake mirrors the
> tragedy of a social system which lives, grows, and prospers by
> material standards alone. (*CM*, 249, 253)

Roy's return from New York is also her salvation. *Beyond Defeat*
opens with her homecoming, bringing with her her fatherless child.
Glasgow's description recalls her own fearful return to One West Main
in the spring of 1916, after her own years away:

> Do we always return to the place where we have suffered most?
> Before she had grasped its meaning, the thought wavered and
> slipped from Roy's mind. She had come back to face life, and life
> had not waited. Of the past, nothing was left but herself and the
> things she remembered. Nothing was here to live down, not even

the bare outline of her old failure. Had the years merely drifted, as
dust drifts without settling, over the house and the street? Yet in
those three vital years, torn up from the deepest roots of her heart,
she had lived and died, and been born over again. . . . (5)

Perhaps one of the greatest similarities between *Vein of Iron* and these
later novels lies in this somber, meditative pace. Glasgow had frequently spoken about the relationship of movement to theme, just as
she had commented expressly on her use of movement in *Vein of Iron*.
Asa's frequent introspection seems to stem directly from the medita-
tions of John Fincastle: the men are nothing alike except in that they
have survived and they feel abandoned by the modern. By the time of
Beyond Defeat, Roy too sounds a great deal like Asa, John, and the rest
of Glasgow's isolated artists. It is Roy who expresses the main theme of
the two novels as she praises her father:

> I want him to have whatever it is that has held you together after
> . . . after you seemed to have lost everything. . . . A strange doctor
> taught me . . . that your life must have a root . . . a living root,
> somewhere. They brought him to see me in the hospital. I think
> they feared, or hoped, I was turning into a mental case. I was so
> low in my mind. . . . He told me, that doctor, I had the sickness—
> or would he have said, disease?—of civilization. He said we were all
> trying to escape from our roots in nature . . . in the simple good-
> ness of living. . . . we could only run round and round, in a circle,
> until we edged nearer a precipice, or came back to win or to lose the
> fight within ourselves. . . . This was when I began to see that my
> help could not come from outside. (125)

Once Roy has learned this, she becomes a survivor—whether or not
she has a husband. Glasgow purposely leaves the outcome of Roy's former romance open to avoid emphasizing any kind of marital answer.
The impact of the fiction should come instead from the characters' reactions to Roy's illegitimate child. The two older women, Lavinia and
Charlotte, cannot accept his existence, but Asa and Kate, "rooted, not
in a decaying tradition, but in nature and in simple goodness of life,"[8]
welcome and love him. In the child's presence lies an important theme:
"Life doesn't stop because it has been broken."[9] "What is the essence,
what is the spiritual quality, that will hold a man together after he has
lost everything else?"[10] Glasgow sees that the real drama lies in the sur-

vival of Asa and Roy, set against a crumbling culture, as her list of ten-
tative titles for *In This Our Life* suggests:

All Things New
Years of Unreason
A Breaking World
The Cloudy Border[11]

It is interesting that her listed titles for the sequel, *Beyond Defeat*, are
much more positive: *While We Live, All the Present, Give Me Tomorrow,
What of the Night*.[12] The explicit titles reflect a tendency toward over-
statement in the late novels; as Glasgow had written in 1941, "There is
always a shock in the discovery that, in print, one must be brutally obvious if one wishes not to be misconstrued."[13]

There seems little reason to question that Glasgow believed in the
philosophy of endurance/survival which her last books expressed; in
her personal writing of the 1940's, however, some sad and even despair-
ing notes exist. From Castine, Maine, 1941: "If only beauty were everything! If only beauty were enough for the mind or the heart!"[14] In 1943:
"For the first time in my long life, I feel that it does not matter whether
or not one writes novels. I spent more than forty years believing that it
mattered greatly, but the contemporary scene and contemporary standards of craftsmanship have destroyed, for me, the faith and the work
of a lifetime."[15] In 1945: "I dread unspeakably the return to Richmond,
and to a house, with the surroundings where I have suffered so deeply."[16]

Many such statements surely reflect Glasgow's anger with the chaos
and waste of war ("I had always felt the vast impersonal anguish of life
more deeply than I had felt my own small—yet vast, too—personal
misery"),[17] but others must be the result of her physical weariness after
years of pain and anxiety: "I had not ever known what it meant to be
well. For many years, I had rarely known what it meant to be free from
pain. The physical labour of writing would be irksome; the mental ha-
rassment might become a slow torture to over-sensitive nerves."[18] This
angst too must be read in the light of her relatively isolated situation in
Richmond: with waning health and wartime travel restrictions, Glasgow's visits to New York and the East coast diminished. One remembers
her earlier complaint to Stark Young, a younger cousin, "How I wish I
could talk over some of it with you! There is not a human being in the
world to whom I might read a chapter, or discuss any part of the work."[19]

Perhaps it is true that during her later life, Glasgow's work with criticism and autobiography countered her sense of isolation. She speaks repeatedly of the importance of her profession, and of her friendships with other writers. Her letters show that intimacy did exist, for her, with such writers and critics as Carl Van Doren, Howard Mumford Jones, Allen Tate, Stark Young, Marjorie Kinnan Rawlings, James Branch Cabell, and many others, and that these friendships were based on respect for each other's writing. In this context, the publication of Glasgow's *A Certain Measure* was important, and she frequently spoke about its preparation in 1942 and 1943.

The collected prefaces are important to Glasgow as well because they gave her a means of creating an identity: Ellen Glasgow, writer. As she grew older, she became especially sensitive about being described as a "Southern" writer or as a "maiden lady." She viewed herself as a distinguished writer, a well-traveled woman rich in both experience and study. In 1941, she took offense at an anonymous reviewer's comment in *Time* that she had lived "a thoroughly conventional spinster's life." Glasgow's asperity is apparent:

> As a matter of verity, the one experience I have never had is the life of a conventional spinster, whatever that is. Or a conventional life of any other nature.[20]

Glasgow's image of herself through the late writing was of a woman who was anything but conventional.

A Certain Measure also allowed Glasgow to write criticism that was more personal than theoretical: she abhorred dry scholarship. As she wrote the prefaces for the novels, she described her work as "a mingling of autobiography and literary criticism" and said of the material, "Much of myself went into that writing. It gave me an opportunity to ramble over my mental universe."[21] That she considered *A Certain Measure* in tandem with *The Woman Within* also seems clear; these were the years of plain speaking, of setting records straight, of justifying her career. Pleased with both books, Glasgow wrote of *The Woman Within*, "My autobiography, even if it requires rather drastic editing in certain chapters, may be the best that was in me."[22]

A Certain Measure was of great importance to Glasgow because it allowed her to describe the art of writing and its centrality to her life: "To disparage an art that one has attempted to practice since the age of seven cannot but seem a gesture wholly theatrical. What honest craftsman . . . would squander a lifetime upon a task that did not contain for him a certain measure of achievement? If I were to deny my life as a writer, it would mean the denial of all that to me has represented reality."[23] Within her prefaces Glasgow sets aright the concept of intellectual creation ("all creative writing is an extension of personality");[24] she confronts the technical problems that arise from the modern reader's interest in "interior worlds"; she insists on the self-determination of form and character. Her descriptions of the way Dorinda Oakley came into being are almost as memorable as the character herself.

And Glasgow turns increasingly, as the book progresses, to the importance of experience. She never brings herself to say, "I could write effectively about joy or heartbreak because I had known it"; rather she refers to the author as *he* and dodges the explicit relationship between herself as woman and the elements of her fiction. It would in fact seem that the thread connecting the prefaces is the notion of novel as portrait of Virginia history. Yet once Glasgow finishes with that somewhat dutiful note, which was originally suggested to her by James Cabell, she writes then about theme, characters, some reality that she too had known. The vigor of *A Certain Measure* is to be found in these later parts of each preface, and in that division is also to be found the paradox of Glasgow's life.

Fifty years too early, Ellen Glasgow was an American woman writer. She knew well that all great novels depend upon "power, passion, pity, ecstasy and anguish, hope and despair,"[25] and as a woman writer she knew the entire gamut. But simply because she was female—and subject to the stereotypes inflicted on women writers—she had to mask what should have been obvious correlations. What should have been a strength became a liability, and even at her most assertive—at the end of her life—she had to title her autobiography *The Woman Within*. Glasgow the writer was—or should have been—somehow unsexed. Only under the mask, inside the writerly disguise, could a woman exist. That Glasgow could at least acknowledge the importance of that woman, regardless of how she had to hide her, is crucial; but we must recognize the difficulty of that acknowledgment if even a writer of Glasgow's stature was slow to make it.

One of Glasgow's chief handicaps in relating aesthetic matters to personal was a diminished vocabulary. Most critics had not recognized any reasonable (or critically respectable) differences between fiction written by men and that written by women. They seemed to believe that all fiction should treat the same kind of characters, the same kind of themes. That Glasgow knew *which* of her novels are best but hesitated to explain why is one index of the critical dilemma. When she recommends novels to a Miss Patterson, her explanations are often misleading.

In this 1936 correspondence, Glasgow first recommends *Barren Ground*, *Vein of Iron*, and *Virginia*, calling them "novels of character." A more accurate description might have been "novels of female character" because all three books show women trapped in a culture unwilling to educate or nurture them to be thinking, independent persons capable of major decisions. The books are powerful; the characterization is splendid, but Glasgow's descriptions of the novels are bland:

> These three novels are concerned with the place and tragedy of the individual in the universal scheme. They treat of the perpetual conflict of character with fate, of the will with the world, of the dream with reality.[26]

This "perpetual conflict" of "character and fate" would be more interesting if it were related to the social position of the female characters. The irony, for the contemporary reader, is that Glasgow nowhere acknowledges that women characters are central to these books.

The slight distinction between what Glasgow calls the "novels of character" and her other choices—*The Romantic Comedians*, *They Stooped to Folly*, and *The Sheltered Life*, books she terms "The Tragicomedy of Manners"—points again to the faultiness of her categories. According to Glasgow, these novels express the "struggle of personality against tradition and the social background." Again, had she said *female* personality, her description would have been more accurate.

With her usual good critical judgment, Glasgow was right in choosing these six novels as her best. She was right in separating them into two triads because the ultimate seriousness of *Barren Ground*, *Vein of Iron*, and *Virginia* did distinguish them from the ironic works. In the serious novels, Glasgow had invested herself. All her knowledge of women's frustration with conventional roles brought Dorinda, Ada, and Virginia to life: these are passionate novels, written with a vehemence that less-concerned fiction—fiction which is less important to the writer—cannot achieve.

The other three novels, those operating more through irony than through involvement, are less intense embroideries on many of the same themes. Judged as skilled writing, these books are satisfying because they so perfectly illustrate narrative existing as theme. They are tidy books, with no extraneous characters or action. They are also less heavily imaged—except for *The Sheltered Life*, which changes from the perfectly controlled ironic novel of manners to the more intense novel of character as Glasgow focuses on Jenny Blair and Eva Birdsong and their similar, difficult problems. It is understandable that Glasgow placed *The Sheltered Life* with *The Romantic Comedians* and *They Stooped to Folly*; she thought of the three novels of manners collectively. A more accurate designation of her great novels, however, would place four books in the category of "novels of character":

> *Virginia*, 1913
> *Barren Ground*, 1925
> *The Sheltered Life*, 1932
> *Vein of Iron*, 1935

The publication dates of these novels tend to confirm that Glasgow found her way to her most successful writing after years of studied apprenticeship. For all she could learn about the craft of great writing, for all her early pleasure at being identified as Harold Frederic with the publication of her first novel, for all her persistence in trying to convey philosophical sophistication, she came to her best writing once she had learned to fuse personal emotion with fictional elements.

She speaks to this point in the preface to *The Miller of Old Church*, when she refers to the 1913 *Virginia* as a stepping stone on her "way to complete freedom." Of the writing of *Barren Ground* Glasgow says that it was a time in which

> I was able to orient myself anew and to respond to a fresh, and, apparently, a different, creative impulse. All that came after this period was the result of this heightened consciousness and this altered perspective. . . . my later way of writing began suddenly, after a long apprenticeship to life, in a single intuitive visitation.[27]

She later observed to Van Wyck Brooks that with *Barren Ground* she "broke away from social history, and allowed my creative impulse to take flight. . . . these later books are more living and more true, I feel, than my earlier novels."[28]

Although the comments elsewhere in the preface are more oblique, Glasgow notes the "top-heavy patriarchal system" that dominated Virginia society and relegated women to the status of slaves or poor whites. She says of traditional Southern novels that, for all their charm, "they lack creative passion and the courage to offend which are the essential notes of great fiction." Great novels must be true to human behavior;

they must begin in a "subjective vision which, together with creative impulse, remoulds a tragic destiny in the serene temper of art." Hesitant she may be, but Glasgow insists on emotional veracity, and she emphasizes that emotions are not the same as ideas. She finally comes to the undefinable, having given up on the repetition of the word *emotion*:

> With the imponderables lies the real force. The universal approach is not without but within; and the way to greatness leads beyond manner, beyond method, beyond movement, to some ultimate dominion of spirit.[29]

Another way of stressing the importance of the self and the psyche is to describe the writer's choice of subjects: "It is the unconscious, not the conscious will that chooses for us our subjects, and over the unconscious we cannot exert prohibitions."[30] As she had written early in *A Certain Measure*, "I wrote solely in obedience to some inward pressure."[31]

"A fan of light, the merest glimmer, unfolds in the darkness." So Glasgow describes the process of coming to fiction/autobiography: "A faint incandescence pricks through the darkness of memory . . . a phosphorescent glimmer . . . an unapprehended sensation."[32] Supported repeatedly by the process of her writing, Glasgow's sense of her becoming a confident woman is movingly retold in *The Woman Within*. From its halting account of her childhood—complete with her dependence on her lovely mother and her fear of her strict father—to the poignant chapters about her first love, her beloved sister's illness and death, and her later romance, Glasgow's autobiography may indeed be "the best that was in her." The control is not only expert; it also creates a voice new to Glasgow. Less stentorian than John Fincastle's, less reminiscent than Asa Timberlake's, the voice of Ellen Glasgow is wistful yet achieving. She wonders about her "dubious identity"; she finds comfort in Jane Welsh Carlyle's admonition that "the heart will stand more breaking than one knew at 25."[33]

Notes for what seems to be an early preface to the autobiography begin, "This quiet book, a journal of the inner life, is not designed for the many who are animated by the will to live and the instinct for happiness, but for the few who, like myself, inherited that strange sense of exile on earth. Essentially, a book of the mind, and a record of intellectual adventure, it is impossible to exclude tides of emotions from any world of the spirit."[34] Emotion, spirit—Glasgow stresses the fragility of impulse, the extrarationality of instinct, of feeling. As she writes later in *The Woman Within*,

One remembers, not with the mind alone. One remembers with the nerves, and the arteries, and the bloodstream long after the mind has defeated and banished the visible images. There are nights, even now, when I am awakened by a drumming along the nerves to the brain. . . . Then, while I am half-unconscious, the ghost of some old unhappiness will rush into my thoughts.[35]

Judged as autobiography, *The Woman Within* is poignant. Its publication places Glasgow in a mainstream of American literary tradition in which the writer works from interior knowledge outward, beginning with the "transfigured experience" of which Glasgow speaks and using that sure knowledge to craft believable characters. Mutlu Konuk Blasing in *The Art of Life* identifies autobiography as peculiarly American and places Whitman, Adams, James, Emerson, Thoreau, and Williams in the list of writers who were primarily autobiographers.[36] Glasgow finds herself in good company. It may well be that she is one of the few women writers to achieve the kind of full consciousness which the use of self-experience as art requires.

For example, when Glasgow describes the death of her mother, and its impact on the person she was then, we too can feel the tremor of the world that "rocked suddenly, and fell to pieces. . . . some other self stands in the center of that desolate room, looks through the blurred windowpanes, and still watches, without knowing what it watches, two sparrows quarreling in the slow rain on the roof. And while I stand there, a mountain of things I had left undone is torn up from the earth, and crashes down on my life" (83–84). The fluid movement between self and other persona, from grief externalized through image to grief internalized through another image forces the reader to both attend and comprehend. The passage is about Glasgow, and yet beyond the merely personal.

Such an occasion gives the reader not only information about Glasgow's life per se but insight into the processes of her dealing with that life. The autobiographical account is an open account; it makes use of history but goes beyond history. In somewhat the same manner, J. R. Raper sees Glasgow's fiction as being concerned with process, with possibility. Glasgow, says Raper, "is more interested in the 'possible' (the 'can be') than in the political, religious, or moral 'imperative' (the 'must be')."[37]

Glasgow's fidelity to what she believes connects both *A Certain Measure* and *The Woman Within* and, more, connects those two books to her fiction. In all her late work, her aims as described in a 1944 note to her literary executors shape her tellings: "I have tried to make a completely honest portrayal of an interior world, and of that one world alone."[38] One must think of Thoreau, requiring "of every writer, first or last, a simple and sincere account of his own life."[39] That aim gives Glasgow's work not only purpose but a sense of gracious dignity. The voice that speaks is a believable one, even if it is one for which we might have wished more traditional happiness. One of the closing paragraphs of *The Woman Within* gives us the Glasgow voice:

> Yes, I have had my life. I have known ecstasy. I have known anguish. I have loved, and I have been loved. With one I loved, I have watched the light breaking over the Alps. If I have passed through "the dark night of the soul," I have had a far-off glimpse of the illumination beyond. For an infinitesimal point of time or eternity, I have caught a gleam, or imagined I caught a gleam, of the mystic vision. . . . It was enough, and it is now over. Not for everything that the world could give would I consent to live over my life unchanged, or to bring back, unchanged, my youth. (296)

To consider Glasgow's writing career finished with the publication of *Vein of Iron* in 1935, as some readers do, would omit consideration of the important *A Certain Measure* and *The Woman Within*, as well as the last novels, which insist that material defeat can lead to personal victory. Glasgow's later books were in some ways very important: without self-consciousness, without obvious artifice, she wrote effectively about the life, problems, and joys of the woman writer. And in this last writing, whether it is focused on Roy Timberlake of *Beyond Defeat* or Ada Fincastle of *Vein of Iron* or Ellen Glasgow of *The Woman Within*, Glasgow creates characterizations of positive, achieving women. The plea of Carolyn Heilbrun for "female characters who are complex, whole and independent" is answered in these characterizations: Glasgow has imagined herself, as she was, accomplished; and she has created women like herself in her countless fictions and nonfictions.[40] As Barbro Ekman has observed,

> In *A Certain Measure* Glasgow had said that she wanted to write a social history of Virginia and it seemed to me that she had indeed done that but that it had turned out to be a history, not of its men, but of its women.[41]

If John Dos Passos and F. Scott Fitzgerald were chroniclers of American life, then Ellen Glasgow can surely be named the chronicler of American women's lives. In her nineteen novels and other writings, she portrayed nearly every kind of woman—from the self-effacing to the aggressive, the Puritanical to the impassioned—and those accurate portrayals have been one of her major contributions to the art of fiction. Glasgow's characterizations have given flesh to the complexity of the female mind and heart, as she grew herself from being a "philosophical" novelist whose first book was credited to a male author to a woman writer whose greatest work—*Virginia, Barren Ground, The Sheltered Life, Vein of Iron,* and *The Woman Within*—came from her own responses to her thoroughly feminine identity. As her fiction clearly records, it was a long journey and a hesitant one. It was also—for readers then and for readers today—an important one.

Notes

I. THE SENSE OF EXILE

1. According to E. Stanly Godbold, Jr., Glasgow's biographer, Glasgow and the Reverend Frank Paradise were engaged from 1907 to 1910, following her affair with "Gerald B.," the mysterious married man she cared for from the turn of the century to 1905. Glasgow's engagement to Henry Anderson began July 19, 1917, and continued several years (*Ellen Glasgow and the Woman Within*).

2. As quoted in the Associated Press sketch of Glasgow, #1831, Box 23 of the Ellen Glasgow Collection, 5060, Alderman Library, University of Virginia. Hereafter cited as University of Virginia. Used with permission of the estate.

3. Erich Kahler, *The Inward Turn of Narrative*, trans. Richard and Clara Winston, pp. 4–5; and Glasgow, "One Way to Write Novels," *Saturday Review of Literature* 11 (December 8, 1934), p. 344, reprinted as preface to *The Sheltered Life* in *A Certain Measure*, p. 193. Hereafter cited as *CM*. See also David J. Gordon's *Literary Art and the Unconscious*.

4. University of Virginia, 5060, Box 23, Associated Press sketch.

5. Carolyn G. Heilbrun, *Reinventing Womanhood*, p. 34. See also Patricia Meyer Spacks, *The Female Imagination*; Adrienne Rich, *Of Woman Born*; Kate Millett, *Sexual Politics*; Ellen Moers, *Literary Women*; Annis V. Pratt, "The New Feminist Criticisms: Exploring the History of the New Space," in *Beyond Intellectual Sexism: A New Woman, A New Reality*, ed. Joan I. Roberts; and Sandra M. Gilbert and Susan Gubar, *The Madwoman in the Attic: The Woman Writer and the Nineteenth Century Literary Imagination*. Useful perspectives are also to be found in *The Lost Tradition: Mothers and Daughters in Literature*, ed. E. M. Broner and Cathy N. Davidson.

6. University of Virginia, 5060, Box 7, notebook 7, p. 13. The title phrase is first used in the Wylie comment and repeated several times. For a recent view of that conflict, see Rosemary Daniell, *Fatal Flowers: On Sin, Sex, and Suicide in the Deep South*.

7. *New York Times*, October 18, 1942; clipping located in University of Virginia, 5060, Box 23.

8. Ellen Glasgow, *The Woman Within*, p. 296. Hereafter cited as *WW*.

9. *CM*, p. 195. Glasgow is pictured as "rebel" by several reviewers, among them Stephen and Rosemary Benét ("Miss Ellen: A Rebel against Regimentation," *New York Herald Tribune* [*Books*], November 17, 1940, p. 7)

and Alfred Kazin ("The Lost Rebel," *New Yorker* 30 [October 30, 1954], p. 130).

10. University of Virginia, 5060, Box 28, to Elizabeth Patterson from Glasgow, 1909.

11. University of Virginia, 5060, Box 7, notebook 7 and unidentified notes.

12. University of Virginia, 5060, Box 5, manuscript draft of *WW*, p. 108. Would have appeared, if used in final version, on p. 130.

13. See Spacks, pp. 145 ff.

14. Glasgow's last fiancé, Henry Anderson, held a commission as colonel and was in charge of the Red Cross Commission to the Balkans from the summer of 1917 to the spring of 1919. She includes him ironically in a list of possible titles and characters which emphasize his political role: "A Red Cross Knight," "Godfrey Plummer Bulfinch," "A Comedy of Cautiousness," "A Predatory turtle dove," "Colonel Godfrey Plummer Bulfinch, who had won his title as a Red Cross decoration and retained it as a political asset" (University of Virginia, 5060, Box 5).

15. University of Virginia, 5060, Box 22.

16. In *The Woman Within*, Glasgow writes that "until one is over sixty one can never really learn the secret of living."

17. University of Virginia, 5060, Box 7, Anderson letter, July 18, 1917.

18. Ellen Glasgow, *Barren Ground*, p. 511. Not only does the novel end with this line but the full closing is even more emphatic: "Dorinda smiled, and her smile was pensive, ironic, and infinitely wise. 'Oh, I've finished with all that,' she rejoined. 'I am thankful to have finished with all that.'" Yet, for all Glasgow's evident seriousness in that ending, some critics have found Dorinda's willingness to live without a companion suspect.

19. Ellen Glasgow, *Letters of Ellen Glasgow*, compiled and edited by Blair Rouse, p. 41. Hereafter cited in text as *L*. Glasgow to Walter Hines Page, Dec. 26, 1902.

20. Godbold, p. 137.

21. Heilbrun, p. 34.

22. Phyllis Chesler, *Women and Madness*; Mary Hiatt, *The Way Women Write*; Elaine Showalter, *A Literature of Their Own*.

23. William W. Kelly recounts these figures from Alice Payne Hackett, *Fifty Years of Best Sellers: 1895–1945* in his introduction to *Ellen Glasgow: A Bibliography*, pp. xv–xvi. The quote from Francis Hackett (whose wife Signe Toksvig became a close friend of Glasgow's in later years) appeared in *Current Literature* 47 (October, 1909), p. 461. As Malcolm Cowley pointed out in "Miss Glasgow's 'Purgatoria,'" *New Republic* 104 (March 31, 1941), p. 441, "No other American novelist was praised so almost universally, exception being made for Willa Cather. No other American novelist was published in two collected editions."

24. University of Virginia, 5060, Box 5, manuscript of *Woman Within*, p. 96; in published version, following p. 113.

25. *CM*, p. 8. Hereafter cited in text.

26. University of Virginia, 5060, Box 7, "Relation of the Scholar to the Creative Arts," p. 5.
27. Tillie Olsen, *Silences*.

2. THE EARLY NOVELS

1. *WW*, p. 40.
2. Julius Rowan Raper, *Without Shelter: The Early Career of Ellen Glasgow*, p. 57.
3. Anne Firor Scott, *The Southern Lady: From Pedestal to Politics, 1830–1930*, p. xi.
4. Ellen Glasgow, *Phases of an Inferior Planet*, p. 88. Hereafter cited in text. I am much indebted to the best study of the female characters in the early novels—Dorothy McInnis Scura's "The Southern Lady in the Early Novels of Ellen Glasgow," *Mississippi Quarterly* 31, no. 1 (Winter, 1977–78), pp. 17–31.
5. Showalter, p. 136.
6. Ellen Glasgow, *The Descendant*, p. 83. Hereafter cited in text.
7. University of Virginia, 5060, Box 1, notes for *Beyond Defeat*.
8. Ellen Glasgow, *The Voice of the People*, pp. 4–5. Hereafter cited in text.
9. The identity of the lover designated as "Gerald B." and the circumstances of their affair remain obscure. Edgar E. MacDonald suggests that the lover was Hewitt Hanson Howland, an editor at Bobbs-Merrill, a man about ten years Glasgow's senior. Although he was married in 1900 when they evidently met, in 1906 he married again to Manie Cobb, sister of Irving S. Cobb. The "end" of his romance with Glasgow, then, would have been his rejection of her in favor of another woman, not his death. MacDonald gives alternate theories in his essay "Biographical Notes on Ellen Glasgow," *Resources for American Literary Study* 3, no. 2 (Autumn, 1973), pp. 249–53.
10. Ellen Glasgow, *The Battle-Ground*, p. 129.
11. Ellen Glasgow, *The Deliverance*, p. xv. Hereafter cited in text.
12. University of Virginia, 5060, Box 6, March 22, 1944.
13. Ibid., letter of January 6, 1945, typed from her handwritten letter.
14. Ibid., Box 5, notebook 3, p. 55.

3. THE YEARS OF LOSS

1. *WW*, pp. 167–68. Again, whether the affair ended so that "Gerald B." might marry someone else, as has been suggested, or in his literal death, the finality for Glasgow would be the same.
2. University of Virginia, 5060, Box 3, notes for *In This Our Life*.
3. University of Virginia, 5060, Box 28, letter to Elizabeth Patterson, August 17, 1909, and another undated letter to her.

4. Ibid., Box 3, notes for *In This Our Life*.

5. Frederick P. W. McDowell, *Ellen Glasgow and the Ironic Art of Fiction*, p. 82.

6. Ellen Glasgow, *The Wheel of Life*, p. 4. Hereafter cited in text.

7. Compare descriptions from *Wheel of Life*, pp. 468–69, and *WW*, pp. 165–67.

8. *WW*, p. 171.

9. Ellen Glasgow, *The Ancient Law*, p. 14. Hereafter cited in text.

10. University of Virginia, 5060, Box 5, notes for *WW*, p. 83; would appear on p. 99 in published version. As McDowell also notes, "With truth she could allege that she did her best work, not when emotion dominated her but when its force had diminished to the throb of remembrance. She had written one of her strongest books, *The Deliverance* (1904), when she was in love with Gerald; but with her deepening love for him and the subsequent agony originating in her renunciation of him and in his death, she sought too conscious a release from emotion. *The Wheel of Life* (1906), *The Ancient Law* (1908), and *The Romance of a Plain Man* (1909), accordingly show her talent at its thinnest. When she was less directly involved, intense emotion did not always result in an artistic impoverishment. For instance, the suffering she experienced as a result of her brother's suicide and her sister's death may well have contributed to the grim force of two of her best books, *The Miller of Old Church* (1911) and *Virginia* (1913)" (p. 31).

11. Godbold, pp. 72–77; see *L.*, pp. 46–50, 52.

12. Ellen Glasgow, *The Romance of a Plain Man*, p. 109. Hereafter cited in text.

13. Ellen Glasgow, *The Miller of Old Church*, pp. 64–65. Hereafter cited in text.

14. Ellen Glasgow, *Virginia*, pp. ix–xx. Hereafter cited in text.

15. *L.*, p. 96.

16. *Battle-Ground*, p. 343.

17. University of Virginia, 5060, Box 9, notebook 8, and as cited in Oliver Steele, "Ellen Glasgow's *Virginia*: Preliminary Notes," *Studies in Bibliography* 27 (1974), pp. 265–89 (quotation from pp. 285–86).

18. Steele, p. 287.

19. Ibid., p. 283.

20. Ibid., p. 283.

21. Ibid., pp. 269, 271.

22. Ibid., p. 269.

23. Grant M. Overton, *The Women Who Make Our Novels*, p. 32.

4. THE YEARS OF THE LOCUST

1. Scott, pp. 222–23.

2. Raper, *Without Shelter*, pp. 241–42.

3. Ellen Glasgow, *Life and Gabriella*, pp. xvii–xviii.

4. Scott, p. 217; Raper, *Without Shelter*, p. 245.
5. Barbro Ekman, "Six Months with Ellen Glasgow in Virginia," *Ellen Glasgow Newsletter*, no. 9 (October, 1978), p. 29.
6. Godbold, p. 99.
7. Overton, p. 32.
8. Ibid., p. 31.
9. Ibid., p. 32.
10. University of Virginia, 5060, especially Box 17; see also letters from Margaret Mitchell and Martha Saxon.
11. *WW*, p. 181.
12. Preface to *Life and Gabriella*, p. xv.
13. Godbold, p. 102.
14. Helen White Papashvily claims in *All the Happy Endings*, p. xv, that a "domestic novel" was "a tale of contemporary domestic life, ostensibly sentimental . . . almost always written by women for women." The center of the book was the home, and common woman was exalted; men were usually disappointing. This critic sees the outgrowth of this kind of fiction as a sign of women's feelings of repression.
15. John Cawelti, *Adventure, Mystery, and Romance*, p. 41.
16. Godbold, pp. 103–104.
17. University of Virginia, 5060, Boxes 9 and 11.
18. Even McDowell, who tends to discount Glasgow's personal life as having been influential in her fiction (p. 9), suggests that the trilogy has some connection with what he calls "her disillusionment with Harold S" (p. 10). He also calls the Anderson engagement "amusing and distressing."
19. University of Virginia, 5060, Box 5, p. 195 in draft of *WW*; would have appeared on p. 243.
20. Ellen Glasgow, *The Builders*, p. 53. Hereafter cited in text.
21. For example, in a letter of December 27, 1916, Anderson compares Glasgow to Dante's Beatrice and describes her as "leading me from the depths of material things to the heights of idealism" (University of Virginia, 5060, Box 9).
22. University of Virginia, 5060, Boxes 9 and 11.
23. Ellen Glasgow, *One Man in His Time*, p. 88. Hereafter cited in text.
24. The epitome of this tendency occurs with Raper's interpretation of Stephen Culpeper as the central character of the novel. Raper describes *One Man in His Time* as "the seduction of a southern Prufrock," although he agrees that most of Glasgow's later novels explore the question, "How is an individual to live best in a world that is not the best of all possible worlds?" That Raper applies that question to a relatively minor character in order to say that Glasgow's attention throughout this period remains trained on male characters appears to be a misreading (see *From the Sunken Garden: The Fiction of Ellen Glasgow, 1916–1945*, pp. 40–50).
25. Richard K. Meeker, Introduction to *The Collected Stories of Ellen Glasgow*. Hereafter cited in text.
26. Overton, p. 33.

27. *Collected Stories*, p. 103.
28. William Kelly, Introduction to "'The Professional Instinct': An Unpublished Short Story by Ellen Glasgow," *Western Humanities Review* 16, no. 4 (Autumn, 1962), p. 302.

5. FINDING OPTIONS

1. Ellen Glasgow, *Barren Ground*, p. 3. Hereafter cited in text.
2. *WW*, p. 192.
3. Rich, p. 246. Monique Parent Frazee points out that Glasgow "never missed" motherhood ("Ellen Glasgow as Feminist," in *Ellen Glasgow: Centennial Essays*, ed. M. Thomas Inge, pp. 174–75). That Parent Frazee couples Glasgow's lack of enthusiasm for children with reservations about warmth in her personal relationships may be misleading, however.
4. Parent Frazee describes Glasgow's motivation as "vengeance" (Inge, ed., pp. 174–75).
5. University of Virginia, 5060, Box 5, notebook 3.
6. See Dorothy Yost Deegan, *The Stereotype of the Single Woman in American Novels*.
7. *CM*, pp. 154–55.
8. *L.*, pp. 74, 107, 69, 118.
9. Ibid., p. 90.
10. *WW*, pp. 245, 244, 243.
11. *L.*, p. 341.
12. *CM*, pp. 177–78.

6. OF MANNERS, MORALS, AND MEN

1. *CM*, p. 211.
2. Ibid., pp. 211, 179.
3. See Godbold, p. 163, and the Anderson letters, University of Virginia. The Marjorie Kinnan Rawlings Collection, University of Florida, provides two comments of interest when one tries to reconstruct Glasgow's emotional profile. Anne Virginia Bennett told Rawlings, who was planning to write the Glasgow biography, "She wrote letters recklessly." Douglas S. Freeman's description of Glasgow was that "she had a succession of violent love affairs that cooled quickly."
4. Ellen Glasgow, *The Romantic Comedians*, pp. 1–2. Hereafter cited in text.
5. Ellen Glasgow, *They Stooped to Folly*, p. 273. Hereafter cited in text.
6. University of Virginia, 5060, Box 5, notes for *They Stooped to Folly*.
7. *CM*, pp. 234 ff.
8. Ibid., p. 237.
9. Ibid., pp. 244–45.
10. Ibid., p. 201.

11. Russel B. Nye, *The Unembarrassed Muse: The Popular Arts in America*, p. 25. For further exploration of this topic, see Ann Douglas, *The Feminization of American Culture*; John Paul Eakin, *The New England Girl: Cultural Ideals in Hawthorne, Stowe, Howells, and James*; and Ernest Earnest's *The American Eve in Fact and Fiction, 1775–1914*.
12. Ellen Glasgow, *The Sheltered Life*, p. 153. Hereafter cited in text.
13. University of Virginia, 5060, Box 21, Glasgow to Maxwell Perkins, August 19, 1937. See also *L.*, pp. 134–35; *CM*, p. 220; and University of Virginia, 5060, Box 14, Glasgow to Miss Patterson, March 4, 1936.
14. University of Virginia, 5060, Box 17, Allen Tate to Glasgow, May 24, 1933.
15. University of Virginia, 5060, Box 14, Glasgow to Dan Longwell, n.d.
16. University of Virginia, 5060, Box 17, Allen Tate to Glasgow, September 9, 1932.
17. *WW*, p. 283.

7. VEIN OF IRON

1. University of Virginia, 5060, Box 14. See also *CM*, pp. 165–69.
2. University of Virginia, 5060, Box 14. As McDowell notes in *Ellen Glasgow and the Ironic Art of Fiction* (pp. 209–10), Fincastle's notions of philosophy are somewhat "sentimental." McDowell finds Glasgow's presentation of the character's beliefs "insubstantial," "contrived," and "inadequate."
3. Ellen Glasgow, *Vein of Iron*, p. 50. Hereafter cited in text.
4. Ibid., p. xv. In *L.*, p. 206, she links *Vein of Iron* and *Barren Ground* as "The Novel of Character" and describes them as being "concerned with the place and tragedy of the individual in the universal scheme. They treat of the perpetual conflict of character with fate, of the will with the world, of the dream with reality." Earlier she refers to *Vein of Iron* as "a companion piece to *Barren Ground*" (p. 107).
5. *Vein of Iron*, p. ix.
6. Ellen Glasgow, "One Way to Write Novels," *Saturday Review of Literature.* 11 (December 8, 1934), p. 344 (see *CM*, p. 193).
7. University of Virginia, 5060, Box 14. Glasgow to Miss Forbes, December 3, 1935.
8. University of Virginia, 5060, Box 14. Glasgow to John Chamberlain, December 2, 1935 (see *CM*, p. 169).
9. University of Virginia, 5060, Box 5, notes for *Vein of Iron*.
10. Raper, *Without Shelter*, pp. 252–53.
11. *CM*, pp. 178–79.
12. Ibid.
13. Ibid.
14. Ibid., p. 181.
15. See a comparable passage in Glasgow's 1938 preface (p. xvii); also *CM*, p. 182. This passage occurs in *Vein of Iron*, p. 46.
16. University of Virginia, 5060, Box 5.

17. *Battle-Ground*, p. 387.
18. Ellen Glasgow, "What I Believe," *Nation* 136 (April 12, 1933), p. 406.

8. THE LAST YEARS

1. *L.*, pp. 177, 184, 179.
2. Godbold recounts the personal support and skirmishes between Glasgow and James Branch Cabell, beginning with his favorable review of *Barren Ground* (pp. 169–72) and continuing through *A Certain Measure* (pp. 233–34).
3. Spacks, p. 231.
4. University of Virginia, 5060, note to Glasgow's literary executors, March 22, 1944; and letter to same, January 6, 1945. See Godbold, pp. 208–11, for full description.
5. *L.*, pp. 281, 280.
6. Ellen Glasgow, *In This Our Life*, p. 467. Hereafter cited in text.
7. Ellen Glasgow, *Beyond Defeat: An Epilogue to an Era*, edited with an introduction by Luther Y. Gore, p. 134. Hereafter cited in text.
8. *L.*, p. 340.
9. University of Virginia, 5060, Box 3, notes for *Beyond Defeat*.
10. *L.*, p. 302.
11. University of Virginia, 5060, Box 3, notes for *In This Our Life*. According to Glasgow (*L.*, p. 276), the title phrase had come from George Meredith's "Modern Love," sonnet no. 50, "When hot for certainties in this our life."
12. University of Virginia, 5060, Box 7.
13. *CM*, p. 249.
14. University of Virginia, 5060, Box 5, *WW* manuscript, p. 250.
15. *L.*, p. 314.
16. Ibid., p. 367.
17. University of Virginia, 5060, Box 5, *WW* manuscript, p. 250.
18. *CM*, p. 247.
19. *L.*, p. 177.
20. Ibid., p. 282.
21. Ibid., pp. 326, 328.
22. Ibid., p. 312.
23. University of Virginia, 5060, Box 2, notes for Foreword, *CM*.
24. *CM*, p. 112.
25. Ibid., p. 148.
26. *L.*, p. 206.
27. *CM*, p. 129.
28. *L.*, p. 339.
29. *CM*, pp. 134, 139, 140, 148.
30. University of Virginia, 5060, Box 7, notes for speech.
31. *CM*, p. 68.

32. University of Virginia, 5060, Box 2, notes for *CM*.
33. Ibid., Box 5, p. 100 and earlier sections.
34. Ibid., Box 7.
35. *WW*, p. 213.
36. Mutlu Konuk Blasing, *The Art of Life: Studies in American Autobiographical Literature*.
37. Raper, *Without Shelter*, p. 248.
38. *WW*, p. v.
39. Henry David Thoreau, *Walden*, ed. J. Lyndon Shanley, p. 3.
40. Heilbrun, p. 34.
41. Ekman, "Six Months with Ellen Glasgow," p. 27.

Bibliography

MANUSCRIPT COLLECTIONS

Ellen Glasgow Collection. Alderman Library, University of Virginia, Charlottesville, Virginia.
Marjorie Kinnan Rawlings Collection. University of Florida, Gainesville, Florida.

BOOKS BY ELLEN GLASGOW

The Descendant. New York: Harper and Brothers, 1897.
Phases of an Inferior Planet. New York: Harper and Brothers, 1898.
The Voice of the People. New York: Doubleday, 1900.
The Freeman and Other Poems. New York: Doubleday, 1902.
The Battle-Ground. New York: Doubleday, 1902.
The Deliverance. New York: Doubleday, 1904.
The Wheel of Life. New York: Doubleday, 1906.
The Ancient Law. New York: Doubleday, 1908.
The Romance of a Plain Man. New York: Macmillan, 1909.
The Miller of Old Church. New York: Doubleday, 1911.
Virginia. New York: Doubleday, 1913.
Life and Gabriella. Garden City, N.Y.: Doubleday, 1916.
The Builders. Garden City, N.Y.: Doubleday, 1919.
One Man in His Time. Garden City, N.Y.: Doubleday, 1922.
The Shadowy Third and Other Stories. Garden City, N.Y.: Doubleday, 1923.
Barren Ground. Garden City, N.Y.: Grosset and Dunlap, 1925.
The Romantic Comedians. Garden City, N.Y.: Doubleday, 1926.
They Stooped to Folly. Garden City, N.Y.: Doubleday, 1929.
The Old Dominion Edition of the Works of Ellen Glasgow. 8 vols. Garden City, N.Y.: Doubleday, 1929–33.
The Sheltered Life. Garden City, N.Y.: Doubleday, 1932.
Vein of Iron. New York: Harcourt, Brace and Co., 1935.
The Virginia Edition of the Works of Ellen Glasgow. 12 vols. New York: Scribner's, 1938.
In This Our Life. New York: Harcourt, Brace and Co., 1941.
A Certain Measure: An Interpretation of Prose Fiction. New York: Harcourt, Brace and Co., 1943.

The Woman Within. New York: Harcourt, Brace and Co., 1954.

Letters of Ellen Glasgow. Compiled and edited by Blair Rouse. New York: Harcourt, Brace and Co., 1958.

The Collected Stories of Ellen Glasgow. Edited by Richard K. Meeker. Baton Rouge: Louisiana State University Press, 1963.

Beyond Defeat: An Epilogue to an Era. Edited with an introduction by Luther Y. Gore. Charlottesville: University Press of Virginia, 1966.

ARTICLES AND UNCOLLECTED STORIES BY ELLEN GLASGOW

"A Woman of Tomorrow." *Short Stories* 29 (May/August, 1895), pp. 415–27.

"No Valid Reason against Giving Votes to Women." *New York Times*, March 23, 1913, sec. 6, p. 11.

"Feminism." *New York Times Review of Books*, November 30, 1913, pp. 656–57.

"Feminism: a Definition." *Good Housekeeping* 58 (May, 1914), p. 683.

"What Is a Novel? A Symposium Showing That It Is More Than 'A Good Story Well Told.'" *Current Opinion* 60 (March, 1916), pp. 198–99.

"Evasive Idealism in Literature." *New York Times*, March 5, 1916, sec. 6, p. 10.

"The Dynamic Past." *The Reviewer* 1 (March 15, 1921), pp. 73–80.

"Mr. Cabell as a Moralist." *New York Herald Tribune (Books)*, November 2, 1924, pp. 1–2.

"Van Doren on Cabell." *New York Herald Tribune*, April 5, 1925, pp. 3–4.

"Ellen Glasgow on Censorship and Sinclair Lewis." *American Library Association Bulletin* 16 (July, 1926), p. 618.

"Preferences of Four Critics, by V. Woolf, G. B. Stern, R. West and E. Glasgow." *New York Herald Tribune (Books)*, April 15, 1928, p. 2.

"Impressions of the Novel." *New York Herald Tribune (Books)*, May 20, 1928, pp. 1, 5–6.

"Some Literary Woman Myths." *New York Herald Tribune (Books)*, May 27, 1928, pp. 1, 5–6.

"The Novel in the South." *Harper's Magazine* 158 (December, 1928), pp. 93–100.

"The Biography of Manuel." *Saturday Review of Literature* 6 (June 7, 1930), pp. 1108–109.

"An Experiment in the South." *New York Herald Tribune (Books)*, March 22, 1931, pp. 1, 6.

"Modern in Tempo and American in Spirit." *New York Herald Tribune (Books)*, January 8, 1933, p. 3.

"What I Believe." *Nation* 136 (April 12, 1933), pp. 404–406.

"Portrait of a Famous and Much Loved Dog." *New York Herald Tribune (Books)*, October 8, 1933, sec. 3, p. 21.

"Memorable Novel of the Old Deep South." *New York Herald Tribune (Books)*, July 22, 1934, pp. 1–2.

"One Way to Write Novels." *Saturday Review of Literature* 11 (December 8, 1934), pp. 344, 350, 355.

"Heroes and Monsters." *Saturday Review of Literature* 12 (May 4, 1935), pp. 3–4.

"Branch Cabell Still Clings to His Unbelief." *New York Herald Tribune (Books)*, October 6, 1935, p. 7.

"George Santayana Writes a 'Novel.'" *New York Herald Tribune (Books)*, February 2, 1936, pp. 1–2.

"Elder and Younger Brother." *Saturday Review of Literature* 15 (January 23, 1937), pp. 3–5.

Of Ellen Glasgow: An Inscribed Portrait. By Ellen Glasgow and James Branch Cabell. New York: Maverick Press, 1938. 16 pp.

"The Deep Past." Excerpt from *The Sheltered Life*, and commentary. In *This Is My Best*, ed. Whit Burnett. New York: Dial Press, 1942.

"Agent and Author: Ellen Glasgow's Letters to Paul Revere Reynolds." Edited by James B. Colvert. *Studies in Bibliography* 16 (1961), pp. 177–96.

"'Nominalism and Realism' by Ellen Glasgow: An Unpublished Essay." Edited by Luther Y. Gore. *American Literature* 34 (March, 1962), pp. 72–79.

"'The Professional Instinct': An Unpublished Short Story by Ellen Glasgow." Edited by William W. Kelly. *Western Humanities Review* 16, no. 4 (Autumn, 1962), pp. 301–17.

BOOKS AND ARTICLES

Adams, J. Donald. "The Novels of Ellen Glasgow." *New York Times Book Review*, December 18, 1938, pp. 1, 14.

———. "Speaking of Books." *New York Times Book Review*, November 24, 1940, p. 2.

———. "Speaking of Books." *New York Times Book Review*, October 30, 1955, p. 2.

Auchincloss, Louis. *Ellen Glasgow.* University of Minnesota Pamphlets on American Writers, no. 33. Minneapolis: University of Minnesota Press, 1964.

Baldwin, Alice M. "Ellen Glasgow." *South Atlantic Quarterly* 54 (July, 1955), pp. 394–404.

Bathwick, Serafine Kent. "Independent Woman, Doomed Sister." In *The Modern American Novel and the Movies*, ed. Gerald Peary and Roger Shatzkin. New York: Ungar Film Library, 1978.

Becker, Allen W. "Ellen Glasgow and the Southern Literary Tradition." *Modern Fiction Studies* 5 (Winter, 1959–60), pp. 295–303.

Benét, Stephen and Rosemary. "Miss Ellen: A Rebel against Regimentation." *New York Herald Tribune (Books)*, November 17, 1940, p. 7.

Blasing, Mutlu Konuk. *The Art of Life: Studies in American Autobiographical Literature.* Austin: University of Texas Press, 1977.

Bond, Tonette L. "Pastoral Transformations in *Barren Ground*." *Mississippi Quarterly* 32 (Fall, 1979), pp. 565–76.

Brickell, Herschel. "Miss Glasgow and Mr. Marquand." *Virginia Quarterly Review* 17 (Summer, 1941), pp. 405–17.

Broner, E. M., and Cathy N. Davidson, eds. *The Lost Tradition: Mothers and Daughters in Literature*. New York: Ungar, 1980.

Brooks, Van Wyck. *The Confident Years: 1885–1915*. New York: Dutton, 1952.

———. *The Writer in America*. New York: Dutton, 1953.

"By a Richmond Girl." Richmond *Dispatch*, June 12, 1897, p. 2.

Cabell, James Branch. *As I Remember It*. New York: McBride, 1955.

———. "The Last Cry of Romance." *Nation* 120 (May 6, 1925), pp. 521–22.

———. *Let Me Lie*. New York: Farrar, Straus, 1947.

———. *Some of Us*. New York: McBride, 1930.

———. "Two Sides of the Shielded," *New York Herald Tribune (Books)*, April 20, 1930, pp. 1, 6.

Cabell, Margaret Freeman, and Padraic Colum, eds. *Between Friends: Letters of James Branch Cabell and Others*. Introduction by Carl Van Vechten. New York: Harcourt, Brace and World, 1962.

Canby, Henry Seidel. "Ellen Glasgow: A Personal Memory." *Saturday Review of Literature* 28 (December 22, 1945), p. 13.

———. "Ellen Glasgow: Ironic Tragedian." *Saturday Review of Literature* 18 (September 10, 1938), pp. 3–4, 14.

———. "*SRL* Award to Ellen Glasgow." *Saturday Review of Literature* 23 (December 28, 1940), p. 3.

Cawelti, John. *Adventure, Mystery, and Romance*. Chicago: University of Chicago Press, 1977.

Chesler, Phyllis. *Women and Madness*. Garden City, N.Y.: Doubleday, 1977.

Chesterman, Evan R. "Her Views of Life." Richmond *Dispatch*, November 30, 1898, p. 5.

"Chronicle and Comment." *Bookman* (New York) 5 (July, 1897), pp. 368–70.

"Chronicle and Comment." *Bookman* (New York) 20 (January, 1905), pp. 402–405.

"Chronicle and Comment." *Bookman* (New York) 24 (January, 1907), pp. 438, 441.

Clark, Emily. "Appreciation of Ellen Glasgow and Her Work." *Virginia Quarterly Review* 5 (April, 1929), pp. 182–91.

Collins, Joseph. "Ellen Glasgow's New Novel: A Tragedy of Old Age." *New York Times Book Review*, September 12, 1926, p. 5.

Cooper, Frederic T. "Representative American Story Tellers: Ellen Glasgow." *Bookman* (New York) 29 (August, 1909), pp. 613–18.

Cowley, Malcolm. "Miss Glasgow's 'Purgatoria.'" *New Republic* 104 (March 31, 1941), p. 441.

———. "A Promise Paid." *New Republic* 113 (December 10, 1945), p. 805.

Dabney, Virginius. "A Prophet of the New South." *New York Herald Tribune Magazine*, August 25, 1929, sec. 12, pp. 6–7, 18.

Daniell, Rosemary. *Fatal Flowers: On Sin, Sex, and Suicide in the Deep South*. New York: Holt, Rinehart, and Winston, 1980.

Davidson, Cathy N. See Broner.

Davidson, Donald. "Another Woman Within." *New York Times Book Review*, January 19, 1958, pp. 7, 14.

Deegan, Dorothy Yost. *The Stereotype of the Single Woman in American Novels.* New York: Octagon Books, 1951, 1969.

DeGruson, Gene. "Addenda to Kelly: Ellen Glasgow." *Papers of the Bibliographic Society of America* 71 (1977), p. 222.

DeVoto, Bernard. *The World of Fiction.* Boston: Houghton Mifflin, 1950.

Douglas, Ann. *The Feminization of American Culture.* New York: Knopf, 1977.

Dunn, N. E. "Ellen Glasgow: The Great Tradition and the New Morality." *College Library Quarterly* 11 (1975), pp. 98–115.

Eakin, John Paul. *The New England Girl: Cultural Ideals in Hawthorne, Stowe, Howells and James.* Athens: University of Georgia Press, 1976.

Earnest, Ernest. *The American Eve in Fact and Fiction, 1775–1914.* Urbana: University of Illinois Press, 1974.

Edel, Leon. "Miss Glasgow's Private World." *New Republic* 131 (November 15, 1954), pp. 20–21.

Ekman, Barbro. *The End of a Legend: Ellen Glasgow's History of Southern Women.* Uppsala: Studia Anglistica Upsaliensia 37, 1979.

———. "Six Months with Ellen Glasgow in Virginia." *Ellen Glasgow Newsletter*, no. 9 (October, 1978), pp. 27–29.

Ewing, Majl. "The Civilized Uses of Irony: Ellen Glasgow." In *English Studies in Honor of James Southall Wilson*, ed. Fredson T. Bowers. Charlottesville: University Press of Virginia, 1951.

Fadiman, Clifton, ed. *I Believe: The Personal Philosophies of Certain Eminent Men and Women of Our Time.* New York: Simon and Schuster, 1938.

Farrar, John. "Publisher's Eye View." *Saturday Review of Literature* 30 (August 9, 1947), pp. 11–12, 26.

Field, Louise M. *Ellen Glasgow: Novelist of the Old and the New South: An Appreciation.* Garden City, N.Y.: Doubleday, 1923.

Fishwick, Marshall W. "Ellen Glasgow and American Letters." *Commonwealth* 17 (January, 1950), pp. 13–14.

Frazee, Monique Parent. See Parent Frazee.

Freeman, Douglas S. "Ellen Glasgow: Idealist." *Saturday Review of Literature* 12 (August 31, 1935), pp. 11–12.

Fremantle, Anne. "The Pursuit of Unhappiness." *Commonwealth* 61 (November 19, 1954), pp. 194–95.

Frey, Christine Elisabeth. "The Evaluation of the Heroine in the Novels of Ellen Glasgow." Ph.D. dissertation, University of Illinois, 1976.

Garland, Hamlin. *Companions on the Trail: A Literary Chronicle.* New York: Macmillan, 1931.

———. "*The Descendant* and Its Author." *Book Buyer* 15 (August, 1897), pp. 45–46.

Geismar, Maxwell. "Ellen Glasgow's Private History." *Nation* 179 (November 13, 1954), p. 425.

————. *Rebels and Ancestors: The American Novel, 1890–1915*. Boston: Houghton Mifflin, 1953.

Gilbert, Sandra M., and Susan Gubar. *The Madwoman in the Attic: The Woman Writer and the Nineteenth Century Literary Imagination*. New Haven, Conn.: Yale University Press, 1979.

Giles, Barbara. "Character and Fate: The Novels of Ellen Glasgow." *Mainstream* 9 (September, 1956), pp. 20–31.

Godbold, E. Stanly, Jr. *Ellen Glasgow and the Woman Within*. Baton Rouge: Louisiana State University Press, 1972.

Golts, Rita R. "The Face of Everywoman in the Writings of Ellen Glasgow." Ph.D. dissertation, Temple University, 1977.

Gordon, David J. *Literary Art and the Unconscious*. Baton Rouge: Louisiana State University Press, 1976.

Gore, Luther Y., ed. *Beyond Defeat*. Charlottesville: University Press of Virginia, 1966.

Gray, Richard. *The Literature of Memory*. Baltimore, Md.: Johns Hopkins Press, 1977.

Gubar, Susan. See Gilbert.

Haardt, Sara. "Ellen Glasgow and the South." *Bookman* 69 (April, 1929), pp. 133–39.

Hackett, Alice Payne. *Fifty Years of Best Sellers: 1895–1945*. New York: Bowker, 1946.

Heilbrun, Carolyn G. *Reinventing Womanhood*. New York: Norton, 1979.

"Henry W. Anderson for Vice-President—The Foremost Anti-Sectionalist and Advocate of a More Perfect Union." (Pamphlet supporting Anderson's candidacy for Republican vice-presidential nomination, 1929.)

Hiatt, Mary. *The Way Women Write*. New York: Teachers College Press, Columbia University, 1977.

Hicks, Granville. *The Great Tradition: An Interpretation of American Literature Since the Civil War*. New York: Macmillan, 1933.

Hoffman, Frederick J. *The Modern Novel in America*. Chicago: Regnery, 1963.

Holland, Robert. "Miss Glasgow's Prufrock." *American Quarterly* 9 (Winter, 1957), pp. 435–40.

Holman, C. Hugh. "Another Look at Nineteenth-Century Southern Fiction." *Southern Humanities Review* 54 (Summer, 1980), pp. 235–45.

————. "April in Queenborough: Ellen Glasgow's Comedies of Manners." *Sewanee Review* 82 (Spring, 1974), pp. 264–83. Included with "*Barren Ground* and the Shape of History" (*South Atlantic Quarterly*, Spring, 1978) in his *Windows on the World: Essays on American Social Fiction*. Knoxville: University of Tennessee Press, 1979.

————. "The Comedies of Manners." In *Ellen Glasgow: Centennial Essays*, ed. M. Thomas Inge. Charlottesville: University Press of Virginia, 1976.

————. "Ellen Glasgow and History: *The Battle-Ground*." *Prospects: Annual of American Cultural Studies* 2 (1976), pp. 385–98. Also in the author's discussion of Glasgow in his *The Immoderate Past: The Southern Writer and History*. Athens: University of Georgia Press, 1977.

————. "The Southerner as American Writer." In *The Southerner as American*, ed. Charles G. Sellers. Chapel Hill: University of North Carolina Press, 1960.

————. *Three Modes of Southern Fiction*. Lamar Memorial Lectures, Mercer University, Macon, Ga., 1965. Athens: University of Georgia Press, 1966.

————. "The Tragedy of Self-Entrapment: Ellen Glasgow's *The Romance of a Plain Man*." In *Toward a New American Literary History: Essays in Honor of Arlin Turner*, eds. Louis J. Budd, Edwin H. Cady, and Carol L. Anderson. Durham, N.C.: Duke University Press, 1980.

Hoskins, Katharine. "The Time of Ellen Glasgow." *Nation* 186 (February 15, 1958), pp. 143–44.

Hubbell, Jay B. "Poe and the Southern Literary Tradition." *Texas Studies in Literature and Language* 2 (Summer, 1960), pp. 151–71.

————. *South and Southwest*. Durham, N.C.: Duke University Press, 1965.

————. *Southern Life in Fiction*. Lamar Memorial Lectures, Mercer University, Macon, Ga., 1959. Athens: University of Georgia Press, 1960.

————. *The South in American Literature, 1607–1900*. Durham, N.C.: Duke University Press, 1954.

————. *Who Are the Major American Writers?* Durham, N.C.: Duke University Press, 1972.

Inge, M. Thomas, ed. *Ellen Glasgow: Centennial Essays*. Charlottesville: University Press of Virginia, 1976.

Jessup, Josephine Lurie. *The Faith of Our Feminists*. New York: Richard R. Smith, 1950.

Jones, Howard Mumford. "Ellen Glasgow: The Earliest Novels." In *A Festschrift for Professor Marguerite Roberts*, ed. Freida Elaine Penninger. Richmond, Va.: University of Richmond Press, 1976.

————. "Ellen Glasgow, Witty, Wise and Civilized." *New York Herald Tribune (Books)*, July 24, 1938, pp. 1, 2.

————. "*In This Our Life*: A Review." *Saturday Review of Literature* 23 (March 29, 1951), p. 506.

————. "Is There a Southern Renaissance?" *Virginia Quarterly Review* 6 (April, 1930), pp. 184–97.

————. "The Regional Eminence of Ellen Glasgow." *Saturday Review of Literature* 26 (October 16, 1943), p. 20.

Kahler, Erich. *The Inward Turn of Narrative*, trans. Richard and Clara Winston. Princeton, N.J.: Princeton University Press, 1973.

Kazin, Alfred. "The Lost Rebel." *New Yorker* 30 (October 30, 1954), p. 130.

————. *On Native Grounds*. New York: Harcourt, Brace and Co., 1942.

Kelly, William W. *Ellen Glasgow: A Bibliography*. Charlottesville: University Press of Virginia, 1964.

Kilmer, Joyce. "'Evasive Idealism' Handicaps Our Literature." *New York Times Magazine*, March 5, 1916, sec. 6, p. 10.

Kristiansen, Marianne. "Work and Love, or How the Fittest Survive: A Study of Ellen Glasgow's *Life and Gabriella*." *Language and Literature* 2 (1973), pp. 105–25.

Lawrence, Margaret. *The School of Femininity*. New York: Stokes, 1936.

Lesser, Wayne. "The Problematics of Regionalism and the Dilemma of Glasgow's *Barren Ground.*" *Southern Literary History* 9 (Spring, 1979), pp. 1–21.

Longest, George C. "A Deep and Loving Heart: The Letters of Amélie Rives to Ellen Glasgow." *Ellen Glasgow Newsletter,* no. 13 (October, 1980), pp. 3–4.

Loveman, Amy. "Ellen Glasgow: A Tribute." *Saturday Review of Literature* 28 (December 1, 1945), p. 26.

MacDonald, Edgar E. "Ellen Glasgow: An Annotated Checklist, 1978–79." *Ellen Glasgow Newsletter,* no. 13 (October, 1980), pp. 15–20.

———. "Ellen Glasgow's Spring Tonic: Blood and Irony." *Richmond Literature and History Quarterly* 1 (1978), pp. 18–27.

———. "An Essay in Bibliography." In *Ellen Glasgow: Centennial Essays,* ed. M. Thomas Inge. Reprinted from *Resources for American Literary Study* 2, no. 2 (Autumn, 1972), pp. 131–56, and 3, no. 2 (Autumn, 1973), pp. 249–53.

———. "The Glasgow-Cabell Entente." *American Literature* 41 (March, 1969), pp. 76–91.

———, ed. *Ellen Glasgow Newsletter,* 1974–82.

McDowell, Frederick P. W. *Ellen Glasgow and the Ironic Art of Fiction.* Madison: University of Wisconsin Press, 1963.

McIlwaine, Shields. *The Southern Poor-White from Lubberland to Tobacco Road.* Norman: University of Oklahoma Press, 1939.

Mann, Dorothea Lawrence, ed. *Ellen Glasgow.* Garden City, N.Y.: Doubleday, 1928.

Marcossan, Isaac F. "The Personal Ellen Glasgow." *Bookman* 29 (August, 1909), pp. 619–26.

Meeker, Richard K., ed. *The Collected Stories of Ellen Glasgow.* Baton Rouge: Louisiana State University Press, 1963.

Mencken, H. L. "New Fiction." *American Mercury* 5 (July, 1925), pp. 382–83.

———. "A Southern Skeptic." *American Mercury* 29 (August, 1933), pp. 504–506.

———. "Two Southern Novels." *American Mercury* 18 (October, 1929), pp. 251–53.

Meyer, Elizabeth Gallup. *The Social Situation of Women in the Novels of Ellen Glasgow.* Hicksville, N.Y.: Exposition Press, 1978.

Millett, Kate. *Sexual Politics.* New York: Avon, 1971.

"Miss Ellen Glasgow." Baltimore *Sun,* April 19, 1903, p. 7.

Moers, Ellen. *Literary Women.* New York: Doubleday, 1976.

Monroe, Nellie E. *The Novel and Society: A Critical Study of the Modern Novel.* Chapel Hill: University of North Carolina Press, 1941.

Murr, Judy Smith. "History in *Barren Ground* and *Vein of Iron*: Theory, Structure, and Symbol." *Southern Literary Journal* 8 (1975), pp. 39–54.

"New Writer." *Bookman* (London) 19 (September, 1900), pp. 167–68.

Nye, Russel B. *The Unembarrassed Muse: The Popular Arts in America.* New York: Dial Press, 1970.

Olsen, Tillie. *Silences.* New York: Delacorte Press/Seymour Laurence, 1978.

Overton, Grant M. *The Women Who Make Our Novels.* New York: Dodd, Mead, 1931.

Papashvily, Helen White. *All the Happy Endings*. New York: Harper and Brothers, 1956.

Parent Frazee, Monique. *Ellen Glasgow: Romancière*. Paris: A. B. Nizet, 1962.

Parker, William Riley. "Ellen Glasgow: A Gentle Rebel." *English Journal* 20 (March, 1931), pp. 187–94.

Patterson, Daniel W. "Ellen Glasgow's Plan for a Social History of Virginia." *Modern Fiction Studies* 5 (Winter, 1959–60), pp. 353–60.

"Portrait." *The Critic* 44 (March, 1904), p. 200.

Pratt, Annis V. "The New Feminist Criticisms: Exploring the History of the New Space." In *Beyond Intellectual Sexism: A New Woman, A New Reality*, ed. Joan I. Roberts. New York: McKay, 1976.

———. "Women and Nature in Modern Fiction." *Contemporary Literature* 13, no. 4 (Autumn, 1972), pp. 476–90.

Quesenbery, W. D. "Ellen Glasgow: A Critical Bibliography." *Bulletin of Bibliography* 22 (May–August, 1959), pp. 201–206; 22 (September–December, 1959), pp. 230–36.

Raper, Julius Rowan. "Ambivalence toward Authority: A Look at Glasgow's Library, 1890–1906." *Mississippi Quarterly* 31 (1977–78), pp. 5–16.

———. *From the Sunken Garden: The Fiction of Ellen Glasgow, 1916–1945*. Baton Rouge: Louisiana State University Press, 1980.

———. "The Landscape of Revenge: *Barren Ground*." *Southern Humanities Review* 13, no. 1 (Winter, 1979), pp. 63–76.

———. *Without Shelter: The Early Career of Ellen Glasgow*. Baton Rouge: Louisiana State University Press, 1971.

Rawlings, Marjorie Kinnan. "Regional Literature of the South." *College English* 1 (February, 1940), pp. 381–89.

Rich, Adrienne. *Of Woman Born*. New York: Norton, 1976.

Richards, Marion K. *Ellen Glasgow's Development As a Novelist*. The Hague: Mouton, 1971.

Richmond, Velma Bourgeois. "Sexual Reversals in Thomas Hardy and Ellen Glasgow." *Southern Humanities Review* 13, no. 1 (Winter, 1979), pp. 51–62.

Rodgers, Audrey T. "Images of Women: A Female Perspective." *College Literature* 6 (Winter, 1979), pp. 41–56.

Rouse, Blair. *Ellen Glasgow*. Twayne United States Authors Series. New York: Twayne Publishers, 1962.

———. "Ellen Glasgow and the Old South." *Saturday Review of Literature* 35 (April 27, 1952), p. 27.

———. "I Remember Miss Glasgow." *Ellen Glasgow Newsletter*, no. 6 (1977), pp. 2–10.

———, ed. *Letters of Ellen Glasgow*. New York: Harcourt, Brace and World, 1958.

Rubin, Louis D., Jr. *No Place on Earth: Ellen Glasgow, James Branch Cabell, and Richmond in Virginia*. Austin: University of Texas Press, 1959.

Santas, Joan Foster. *Ellen Glasgow's American Dream*. Charlottesville: University Press of Virginia, 1965.

Schmidt, Jan Zlotnik. "Ellen Glasgow: An Annotated Checklist, 1973–

Present." *Ellen Glasgow Newsletter*, no. 9 (1978), pp. 1–14.

Scott, Anne Firor. *The Southern Lady: From Pedestal to Politics, 1830–1930*. Chicago: University of Chicago Press, 1970.

Scura, Dorothy McInnis. "Glasgow and the Southern Renaissance: The Conference at Charlottesville." *Mississippi Quarterly* 27, no. 4 (Autumn, 1974), pp. 415–34.

———. "The Southern Lady in the Early Novels of Ellen Glasgow," *Mississippi Quarterly* 31, no. 1 (Winter, 1977–78), pp. 17–31.

Showalter, Elaine. *A Literature of Their Own*. Princeton, N.J.: Princeton University Press, 1977.

Spacks, Patricia Meyer. *The Female Imagination*. New York: Avon, 1976.

Steele, Oliver. "Ellen Glasgow's *Virginia*: Preliminary Notes." *Studies in Bibliography* 27 (1974), pp. 265–89.

Stineback, David C. "'The Diminished Grandeur of Washington Street': Ellen Glasgow's *The Sheltered Life*." In his *Shifting World: Social Change and Nostalgia in the American Novel*. Lewisburg, Pa.: Bucknell University Press, 1976.

Stone, Grace Z. "Ellen Glasgow and Her Novels." *Sewanee Review* 50 (July–September, 1942), pp. 289–301.

Tate, Allen. "The New Provincialism: With an Epilogue on the Southern Novel." *Virginia Quarterly Review* 21 (Spring, 1945), pp. 262–72.

Thoreau, Henry David. *Walden*, ed. J. Lyndon Shanley. Princeton, N.J.: Princeton University Press, 1971.

Tindall, George B. *The Emergence of the New South, 1913–1945*. History of the South Series, no. 10. Baton Rouge: Louisiana State University Press, 1967.

Trigg, Emma Gray. "Ellen Glasgow." *Woman's Club Bulletin* (Richmond, Va.) 11, no. 2 (1946).

Tutwiler, Carrington C., Jr. *Ellen Glasgow's Library*. Charlottesville: University Press of Virginia, 1967.

Van Auken, Sheldon. "The Southern Historical Novel in the Early Twentieth Century." *Journal of Southern History*, 14 (May, 1948), pp. 171–86.

Van Doren, Carl. "*Barren Ground*." *New Republic* 42 (April 29, 1925), p. 271.

Van Gelder, Robert. "An Interview with Miss Ellen Glasgow: A Major American Novelist Discusses Her Life and Work." *New York Times Book Review*, October 18, 1942, pp. 2, 32.

Van Vechten, Carl. *Fragments from an Unwritten Autobiography*, vol. 2. New Haven, Conn.: Yale University Press, 1955.

Villard, Leonie. "L'Oeuvre d'Ellen Glasgow, romancière americaine." *Revue Anglo-Americaine* 11 (December, 1933), pp. 97–111.

Wagenknecht, Edward. *Cavalcade of the American Novel*. New York: Holt, 1952.

Wellford, Clarence. "The Author of *The Descendant*." *Harper's Bazaar* 30 (June 5, 1897), pp. 458, 464.

Westbrook, Perry D. "Ellen Glasgow and William Faulkner: Vestigial Calvinism and Naturalism Combined." In his *Free Will and Determinism in Ameri-*

can Literature. Cranbury, N.J.: Associated University Presses, 1979.

Wilcox, Louise Collier. "Ellen Glasgow." Boston *Evening Transcript*, February 17, 1904, p. 17.

Wilson, Edmund. *Patriotic Gore: Studies in the Literature of the American Civil War*. New York: Oxford University Press, 1962.

Wilson, James Southall. "Ellen Glasgow: Ironic Idealist." *Virginia Quarterly Review* 15 (January, 1939), pp. 121–26.

――――. "Ellen Glasgow: 1941." *Virginia Quarterly Review* 17 (April, 1941), pp. 317–20.

――――. "Ellen Glasgow's Novels." *Virginia Quarterly Review* 9 (October, 1933), pp. 595–600.

Wittenberg, Judith B. "The Critical Fortunes of *Barren Ground*." *Mississippi Quarterly* 32 (Fall, 1979), pp. 591–609.

Young, Stark. "Beautiful Apologia." *New Republic* 109 (October 25, 1943), pp. 588–91.

――――. "Prefaces to Distinction." *New Republic* 125 (June 7, 1933), pp. 101–102.

Index